Crappy to Happy

A Practical Guide for Finding Happiness

By Brett J. Novick, LMFT

TRAIN OF THOUGHT
PRESS

Publisher's Note

This book is designed to provide information and motivation to our readers. It is sold with the understanding that the publisher is not engaged to render any type of psychological, legal, or any other kind of professional advice. No warranties or guarantees are expressed or implied by the publisher's choice to include any of the content in this volume. Neither the publisher nor the individual author shall be liable for any physical, psychological, emotional, financial, or commercial damages, including, but not limited to, special, incidental, consequential, or other damages. Our views and rights are the same: You are responsible for your own choices, actions, and results.

ISBN: 978-0-9861485-8-3
Library of Congress: 2018933520
TOTP: C2HBN03072018
Summary: Therapist gives advice on how to be happy.

Connie Johnston

Train of Thought Press

2275 Huntington Drive, #306

San Marino, CA 91108

TRAIN OF THOUGHT
P R E S S

www.TrainOfThoughtPress.com

Table of Contents

Dedication:..i
Other Books By Brett J. Novick:.............................iii

Preface: 4
Chapter 1: You & Your Life....................................12
Chapter 2: Technology & Your World....................91
Chapter 3: You And Others... Relationships From *Crappy To Happy*: 104
Chapter 4: You And Long-Term Partnerships.......131
Conclusion:..145
About The Author:...148

Dedication:

I would like to dedicate this book to my late father, Dr. William Novick, who taught me how to be a father. To my parents who taught me the importance of hard work and values. My wife, Darla, who teaches me each and every day how to be a better person, parent, and spouse, and provides me infinite happiness. My children, Billy and Samantha, who give me hope for a future generation with pride and joy. Also, to the many students, parents, and educators that I have had the honor of working with over the years who have taught me so very much. Please know, I was honored to be allowed to play a small part in their lives, the many mentors who in both education and life inspired me in every aspect of my own life. Finally, a heartfelt thank you to the publishers and staff at Train of Thought Press for your confidence in publishing this book, and to you, the reader, for taking precious time out of your schedule to read it. Thank you.

OTHER BOOKS
BY BRETT J. NOVICK:

- *Parents and Teachers Working Together*

- *The Likeable, Effective, and Productive Educator*

- *The Balanced Child: Teaching Children Social Skills & Character Building*

- *Brain Bullies: "Standing Up to Anxiety & Worry"*

- *Don't Marry a Lemon*

Preface:

They say you can tell a lot about a person from what they read. If that is the case, I should be a living self-help library. I have always been interested in how people work, why they do what they do, and how I can improve myself by helping others to reach their optimum lifestyle.

More times than I would like to count, I fail at reaching my emotional best. I blame others over little things, I beat myself up versus making productive choices, or I allow myself to be lazy when I know it is best for neither my physical nor emotional health.

I tell you this because you must understand that none of us are even close to perfect, and we need the ability not only to grow and realistically develop into our best selves, but also to forgive ourselves sincerely when we so often come up short. I have been a therapist for almost two decades and want to believe I have helped many people. But here's a little secret—many people go into counseling seeking to discover more about themselves as well.

After years of talking to countless people of all ages and cultures, and in a host of situations, I have recognized that many of us (accidentally or purposefully) step in the "piles" of manure in the pastures of our lives. Some of us wipe our feet off and keep moving, while others drag the stench wherever we go and don't fully understand why people move away from us as a result.

This book is for you, and selfishly for me, too (if I am honest). It is a reminder of what we all can do to keep from continually dragging the *crap* under our feet when doing the unpleasant work to scrape it off might bring us greater joy in the long run. It is about what I have found that may be useful for each of us to remember.

I ask you to keep an open mind, read, and reread any parts of the book you find that may pertain especially to you. The book is designed so that each "pile," if you will, is sectioned for you to read according to your respective situation. Sometimes, I find the most difficult task to do in our fast-paced, quick-solution-driven world is to simply sit down and take precious time to read a book. Consequently, I skim, I highlight, I skip over pages or just put the whole thing down altogether. I hope this format allows our time together to be useful, if that is indeed the case, because you can pinpoint what interests you or come back to specific sections as necessary.

Furthermore, *Crappy to Happy* is divided into a few segments that I believe most pertain to the spectrum from *crappiness* to *happiness* in our lives: you (what you think about yourself), others (relationships and their influence on your life), technology (internet partnerships and their impact on you), and others (a catch-all for those slippery topics that don't seem to quite fit anywhere else and fall through the proverbial cracks).

Probably the most important aspect of learning anything new is not simply in casual reading. After all, I can *read* another language on paper by sounding out the words clumsily—it does not mean I *understand* what I have read. No, it takes more—it involves comprehending, trying, retrying and, finally, application.

Nothing—and I mean nothing—whether it is counseling, your best friend's greatest advice, reading, or life coaching will work unless you assimilate the information and apply it regularly. If you take information and put it up to collect dust on your shelf, it will not help (no matter how good or applicable it is). Should you want more or get different results, break the cycle and do something smart, practical, and different. We all tend to get into slumps and, as Dr. Seuss says best in *Oh, The Places*

You'll Go, "Unslumping yourself is not easily done."[1] Doing something positive to break out of a cycle of negativity can only come from you, and no-one else. At times it means doing something subtly—at other junctures, it means executing something far greater. For many, it is difficult, and not everyone may respond to your change favorably. Not everyone likes a new you when the old one was as comfortable and nice as a worn-in pair of shoes. If you don't change, you are predictable, and there is no fear of you outgrowing present stale relationships or requiring others to change or adapt.

Why the Title *Crappy to Happy*?

Our world has become a universe of sound bites. Think about it—we now use emoticons to substitute for complex feelings in one tiny picture on the bright glow of a smartphone. Our world is no longer one of extended conversations and communication. It is now one in which a few flicks of your thumbs suffice for the musings of deep thoughts and exchanges between two people.

---

[1] "Oh, The Places You'll Go! Quotes by Dr. Seuss." *By Dr. Seuss*, www.goodreads.com/work/quotes/2125304-oh-the-places-you-ll-go.

So, the title *Crappy to Happy*? We use a new library of emoticons from feeling *crappy* to *happy*, in our new lexicon of virtual conversation. Our world no longer has the patience for the extended back-and-forth of interaction from yesteryear. Listening faces a real danger of extinction as well in our new web-based existence. Technology is now usurping the dialogue which generation upon generation has developed as bonds with which to support and connect one to another.

That is enough about technology—all of us have embraced this new world to one degree or another, and its aspects can be far more positive than negative. What we are going to discuss in this book, dear reader, is something far more vital. How do we make progress, or scrape away those piles of "*crappy*" and turn our existences more toward that yellow, shining emoticon of "*happy*"? This is a vital and integral question for which we seek to find an answer.

For many, the space between *happy* and *crappy* seems infinitely wide. It is always out of one's grip, like trying to hold a lathered bar of soap that slips and slides out of your hands. The harder you grasp it, the slicker and more slippery it becomes, and the more it seems to jump and slither. A look at the *Harris Poll Happiness Index* number for society is currently only

31 out of 100. That figure was at 34 in 2016 and has hovered in the low- to mid-30s since Harris began calculating it in 2008. Indeed, happiness can seem an elusive mirage that skirts past many of us in modern society.[2]

This book is not intended to be long on theory. It is a collection of things I have found either support or stand in the way of happiness after my twenty years as a therapist, father, friend, and human being. It serves as a reminder for me when I enter the dark, stinky cellar of my own *crap* to prompt myself that we all must keep our eyes focused on the horizon, for that is where the *happier* sunrise ahead always is. It is easier, of course, to not look toward the blindingly bright sunshine of the present and future, and instead look down at the crap that seems to pile up all around you. When you do, though, what you miss is the warmth of life that shines down upon your face.

This book will, hopefully, make you laugh somewhat. However, it is mostly intended to be direct and friendly... but frank. We all deserve to

---

[2] Poll, The Harris. "Older Americans, Those Who Are Religious, and Even Political Party Members Are Happier." *Health & Life*, www.theharrispoll.com/health-and-life/2015_Happiness_Index.html.

seek and find happiness, provided it does not impede the rights of others in society. How important is happiness in the world? In a research study of more than 10,000 people from 48 countries, psychologists Dr. Edward Diener of the University of Illinois at Urbana-Champaign and Dr. Shigehiro Oishi of the University of Virginia found that people from a multitude of countries and cultures valued the trait of happiness as being more vital than any other goal presented in their lives.[3] Think about that for a moment. Everyone around the world seems to agree on one single thing—the elusive search for happiness.

Let's start stepping over the piles of crap within ourselves, with others, at work, and on the web. Doing so will help you avoid dragging the stink of your challenges from situation to situation on the sole (or soul) of your shoe. Thus, your life is one filled with happiness versus the foul stench of crappiness.

I want to be clear about one vital element—that this book is not a substitute for counseling or professional

---

[3] "In Poor Nations, Less Satisfaction But More Meaning In Life." *Psych Central News*, 6 Oct. 2015, psychcentral.com/news/2013/12/19/in-poor-nations-less-satisfaction-but-more-meaning-in-life/63520.html.

help. Sometimes we procrastinate, hesitate, or feel ashamed when we ask for professional assistance. As a counselor, I have sought counseling in the past and would seek it again in the future if needed. Never let pride, fear, or anxiety get in the way of you being the best you or gaining the help you may need. We often need others to get through what we cannot handle alone.

Chapter 1: You & Your Life

"Make the most of yourself...
for that is all there is of you."
— ***Ralph Waldo Emerson***

Let's start with the beginning: *you*. After all, that is the most important subject of this book—simply you.

You might say, "Who, me? No, nothing special here—I am just a person who does their job, takes care of their family, and, well… that's it." But that is precisely what makes you special. Hear me out—it is not some huge accomplishment or promotion that determines a person's value. Rather, it is the tiny, day-to-day ways you cumulatively handle life and treat others that are etched into the memories of those around you. As actress Audrey Hepburn so beautifully phrased, "You may only be just one person, but to one person you may be the world."

Of course, you may be someone who summarily dismisses any statement of how special you are as some psychological self-help mumbo-jumbo. In this world, we are often taught not to brag or boast about ourselves. While there may be a great deal of validity in this, it is also just as wrong to go to the other extreme and be your own worst enemy via putting yourself down, criticizing yourself constantly, and trying to never utter a positive word about yourself. Why is it acceptable to do the latter and not okay to do the former?

The unfortunate fact of the matter is that we are often our own harshest and worst critics. We are far more critical of ourselves than anyone else could possibly be or than we would tolerate from another toward ourselves. It is often easier to use the proverbial whipping belt of judging ourselves before anyone else has a chance to do it. We whip ourselves thoroughly with that belt and use our thoughts to strike at our fragile egos over and over again. Further, we harness our own anxiety and worry to create a cycle that sends our self-esteem swirling down and into our own thought toilet of *crappiness*.

We often believe that being a martyr is what we are supposed to do. We become perpetual victims to our jobs, our family, our friends, or all of the above. We give and give until we have nothing left, and then… we give some more. Our lives are ruled by schedules or others' expectations and desires. And what is the very last item on that list? Our needs, wants, and health.

Obviously, one must place their family and jobs high on the life priority list—however, we often forget the "me" on the radar of our lives. When do you have time to reflect on yourself? Is it when you are too tired emotionally or physically to do anything but sleep or stare blankly into the television, at the reflection of your existence?

Loom around the world—nature seeks a constant sense of balance. Similarly, your life was meant to have some balanced homeostasis. Now, you may say, "I don't have time for balance." Who sets your time for the twenty-four hours in a day? You choose who (or what) controls your life, either by your actions or a lack thereof. You fill your days based upon the desires of others, and it is you who leaves nothing in the proverbial tank of life for yourself. If you let others control the precious commodity of your time, I promise they will do so happily and exhaust it all.

Additionally, when you live only based on a daily, day-to-day existence, you are only doing just that— existing. You fail to create a mission or vision for yourself because you are just surviving and never thriving. If I were to tell you that you needed to get somewhere, your initial questions may be such as: "What are the directions? Where is my GPS? How do I get there?" Well, if you do not know where you want to go or have a map to get there, how do you know when you've arrived, or even when you should expect to get there?

I hope that this chapter answers some of those questions. At the very least, it will set you on your way toward the general direction you want to take. Remember that self-centeredness and selfishness are two very different concepts. Self-centeredness is a vital survival life skill. If many people depend on you, you must be self-centered. Why?

When you get a new tire on your car, you trust that the mechanic is firmly installing that tire on your vehicle. Why? Because you don't want it flying off at 60 mph and causing you to lose control of your vehicle. Imagine you are the center of that wheel and those important to you are the spokes. When the test of life spins you around, if you are not firmly grounded, who will be there to keep those spokes from flying off into oblivion?

Pile #1
Comparing Yourself to Others

Here is a little information that you may not know: We all have issues—we _all_ do. Yours may be different from mine, but all of us have numerous imperfections. Now, we generally try not to highlight ours to the world. Why would we? Many of us have a high degree of shame or embarrassment that stops us from accepting the flaws that make us, well... human. Yet, they are there, and we are well aware of them, like a glowing neon sign with an arrow buzzing and flashing down constantly upon our fragile psyche. Even when they may not seem as obvious to others, we know they are right there, glaringly in front of us.

I tell you this because often we compare ourselves to others and quietly emphasize our own faults and blemishes. Hence, we tend not to recognize that the person looking back at us has many of the same issues and/or insecurities as we do, hidden and distorted through their own mask of false self-confidence. However, like you, that person avoids discussing these proverbial kinks in their own armor for fear of emotional injury.

For example, do you notice that you often will say things to your spouse, boyfriend/girlfriend, or children that you would never say to others? You may be the kind of person who unloads on them verbally, stating what you would not say to a stranger on the street and, in the same breath, shares loving things that you would likewise not say to those you encounter in public. That freedom to be who you are and take off that social mask you wear out in the world is kept under the roof of your home.

So, the comparison we make with others is often inaccurate because we cannot possibly look at others from an accurate perspective. What you see on the surface of a person, in their life, or in their household may be very different from what is on the inside. When you look at a person openly and honestly, you see them warts and all (and that is not such a bad thing—it is what makes us who we are).

Many keep a poker face on throughout life and avoid showing their weaknesses and fears. We do so with the shaky belief that we will lose the game of life if we show our emotional hand of cards.

Pile #2
Believing You Are Owed Something/Anything

This is a very similar "pile" to comparing yourself to others and/or thinking life to be unfair. Neither the world nor your parents/family owe you anything. If you are lucky, and your parents provided you with love, food, and shelter... that is it. Any other things—such as loans, inheritance, gifts, support—those are a bonus.

If you spend your life wallowing because you were not given something to which you thought you were entitled, you will waste your days with that bitterness. Yes, you have not been given what you may have been owed—however, would you like to spend your life trying to fill that void with resentment? Or would you prefer to fulfill your life by earning what you want independently, on your own terms, and without invisible strings attached? The latter is far sweeter and more enjoyable than the former, and provides true freedom and self-satisfaction.

Pile #3
Not Worrying About Your Health

Think of the last time you felt really sick. I mean your head throbbed, your throat felt like sandpaper, and chills and rushes of heat were hitting you at the same time. If you remember that, you probably also remember begging to feel better. Then when you did, you moved on with your hectic lifestyle, leaving the illness in the dust.

Probably the most vital element of one's happiness is one's own health. If you are feeling *crappy* physically, you cannot possibly be fully *happy*. Take care of yourself, and the most crucial part of your happiness will be fulfilled.

This includes the following tasks (some may be common sense but are also, conversely, the easiest to overlook):

- Be certain to go to your physician and get physicals regularly.
- Exercise according to your medical professional's guidance.
- Eat healthy and regular meals.
- Make certain to get enough sleep.
- Take care of your mental and physical health.

Pile #4
Not Having a Definitive Purpose

Holocaust survivor and psychiatrist Dr. Victor Frankl wrote the legendary book, *Man's Search for Meaning*. In the tragedy and despair that was the Holocaust, his worldview should have been one of pessimism and fear tinged with deep self-pity and thoughts of sheer victimization. Yet, he held onto a singular constant hope and light—a search for meaning in his daily life of despair. In fact, he took his experiences and developed a whole theory of counseling called Logotherapy (the goal of this theory is in finding a specific meaning for one's life and existence).[4] Better phrased by Dr. Frankl, "Everything can be taken from a man but one thing: the last of the human freedoms—to choose one's attitude in any given set of circumstances, to choose one's own way."

If you have ever been to a meeting in which there is no agenda nor discernible objective, you will understand the frustration of not having a purpose. The group meets and meanders aimlessly from one topic to another, frustration builds, and the conversation ends right where it started—without getting anything done. In short, without knowing where you want to go, you simply go nowhere and cycle into apathy and frustration.

Some Ideas for Finding a Purpose:

- Don't Live in A Bubble: Comfortable is not always good. Comfortable keeps you doing the same things and getting the same results. Ask yourself first, "What do I want?" Don't just say, "I don't know if I can do that," or "That is not me." Brainstorm outside the box of your usual thinking.

---

[4] Frankl, Viktor E. *Man's Search for Meaning*. Woodside Terrace Kiwanis Club, 1980.

- Think Outside of Yourself: That *crappiness* feeling is often isolating, or people who feel crappy isolate (it is a "chicken or the egg" scenario). Either way, thinking outside yourself through volunteering or some other philanthropic activity can lead to happiness.

- What excites you? Dig deep—what would you do, even if you were not paid? What is your passion? This may well direct you toward your life's purpose.

- Look for a spiritual/religious purpose: Seeking a purpose outside yourself serves to center and ground you. These roots can anchor you when the storms of life try to blow you off track or fog your priorities.

- Where do your talents lie? Often your talents naturally lead you down the road to the purpose of your existence. None of us are talented at everything, but all of us have a talent or penchant at something.

- Do you have more than one passion? If you are lucky, perhaps your passion straddles more than one item. Seek these out. If you are bored in life it may be because you are bored in what you seek within the confines of your comfort zone—a comfort zone that is suffocating your ability to reach your fullest potential.

Pile #5
Believing Life is Fair

As children, we believed "fair" was universally equated with "equal". If my sibling were to get something, I was to get something as well. If my sibling were to get candy at the local convenience store, so was I. If my brother were to get a new toy at the toy store, I would, too. If my sister got that frilly pink size 0 dress at the mall, I was entitled to one, too.

What is that you say? You don't fit into a size 0? You're a guy who doesn't wear dresses? You don't like frills? Then I guess the concept of "one-size-fits-all" fairness does not fit into your narrow stereotypes of what fairness is about. Life does not work in a linear way, wherein everyone gets treated the same way, at the same time, with the same thing. Nor should it.

Each of us have specific needs at specific times. What you need now may be vastly different from what you need in the future. Now, you can howl and cry about how life is unfair and you are being treated unjustly. The more vital question is, what do you do about it?

Chapter 1: You & Your Life

Many of us often waste time contemplating how life is not fair, and flush ourselves into a toilet spiral of crappiness in which we take ourselves to a dark place deep within the recesses of our mind. It is as though we are on a treadmill of our own making. We do a lot of running in our head, but in the end, we are back where we started.

Let's take a look at the various insidious "piles" in the yard of unfairness:

- My Parents Did Not Treat Me Well and Caused Me to be Like This:

   True, as a child you have little control over the world that surrounds you. Adults control what you eat, what you wear, even when you use the bathroom. Don't believe me? Take a child to a restaurant and ask them if they need to use the bathroom. They will swear up and down that they do not. That is, until the food comes. Now they can control the adult in a passive-aggressive manner by having them get up, leave their food and company, and go to the bathroom.

   As an adult, however, the tables are turned. You are now in charge of yourself. You have as much control over your life as the next person. Your time can be spent ruminating and looking back at your childhood or looking forward. Yes, it is unfair that you were not provided with the childhood you may have wanted. Maybe you didn't have what your neighborhood, cousin, or sibling had.

You may not have the parent that you wanted or deserved. Perhaps they simply could not offer those things to you because of their own limitations (one of the things you begin to realize as you mature is that our parents are not perfect and have shortcomings of their own). Now, you are left with choices to make going forward. If you feel you were abused or neglected as a youth, then think of the power you continue to give that person now as an adult by wasting another minute, hour, day, or year of your life by allowing them to monopolize the most precious recesses of your mind.

If you didn't like how you were parented, use that as a yardstick to learn what you don't want to do as well as what you *do* want to do. Ask yourself, "How do I want to parent myself in my life? How do I want to parent my children (now or in the future)?" In short, you learn just as much—if not more—from poor role models as you do from positive ones. Though most of us wish we had the positive ones to model from, as opposed to the poor ones.

- Seeking Material Things as a Means of Happiness:

Imagine for a moment your dream car. I'm not talking the car you can afford... I mean your dream car—every feature, the perfect color and model. With that new 2019 model, you are the envy of everyone. When you drive down the street, all eyes are on you and the sportster that is the luxury machine of everyone's fantasies.

For a few wonderful months, you bask in the admiration of those around you. You are the one everyone looks to on the road as the standard of success and materialistic glory. Then, you see the most horrible sight—the 2020 model of your car that has better features, a stronger engine, and the color palette that you were secretly hoping would have adorned your car. You are heartbroken as you no longer have the best car on the block and the eyes of adoring admirers now shift to someone else.

So it is with having a better smartphone, a bigger television, nicer clothes, more money. It is a bottomless pit. If you look to materialism for happiness, you will be left with a relentless hunger that can never be fed by the empty "fast food" lifestyle that is found in the seeking of a better car, bigger house, or better clothes. You will never meet your goal—it is always just out of reach, and so is the peace that comes with being satisfied.

Pile #6
Your Thinking is Stinking (A Quick Review/Synopsis)

Our minds are constantly churning. We are like overloaded computers, with a hard drive light that is always flickering and flashing as thoughts ping and dart through our heads like the shooting chrome ball in some eccentric game of pinball. We are always thinking about today, tomorrow, and yesterday.

The quality of those thoughts is vital. Are they accurate? Are they helpful or useful? Do they allow us to form a clear and accurate perception of the world that surrounds us?

When they are/do not, they are often called cognitive distortions. These are thoughts that are magnified, disfigured, or otherwise manipulated in a manner that is not useful to one's own emotional well-being. They are optical illusions within our brain, yet seem very real.

Let's Look at the Most Common Elements of "Stinking Thinking":

- "Filtering:" Each morning when you make coffee, you take out the used filter and then throw out the discarded sludge that is the leftover coffee grounds before you drink your cup of Joe, right? You are not likely to slurp down the muddy, discarded mess of ground coffee in the filter.

  Yet, in filtering, you are essentially doing a similar thing with your thought process. You filter out all the positive thoughts and tend to exaggerate the negative ones. It is like you walk around letting the negative aspects of life stick in the crevices of your brain to grow and fester, while those positive elements of your day are efficiently expelled into the air and neither experienced nor appreciated.

- "Black-and-White" Thinking: Many of us tend to be colorblind when it comes to our own thinking. We think that most facets of our life are at either one extreme or another. In reality, most elements of your life exist along a gray spectrum of many shades. Stop looking at your experiences as being one way or another (i.e. "I totally failed/succeeded"). In truth, it is invariably more complicated than that. Look for the gradations that indicate how much success is made in a particular venture, rather than thinking in extremes. Look for the "good enough" versus the perfection that always seems just out of reach. This is more accurate and useful.

- "Generally Generalizing": Often we take one sliver of an experience to represent the whole. For instance, you try one type of Italian food or go on a single ride at an amusement park and decide, based on that one limited encounter, "I don't like Italian food or amusement rides (prior to looking at the bigger picture of other foods, rides, etc.)." One experience does not accurately portray the whole.

- "Conclusion Jumper": Often we make a broad conclusion based on minimal information. The challenge lies within the fact that many of us seem wired to making conclusions tending toward the negative on those precious few details. So, with limited accurate information, we make a quick decision. Ask questions and learn more details before you jump to that *crappier* conclusion in your mind.

- "The Sky Is Falling!": Some of us live in a perpetual state of fear that the worst thing is always bound to happen. The words in our head usually begin with, "What if?" We let those "what-ifs" get out of control, and even the tiniest issue becomes a monumental issue of life-or-death proportions. Not everything is a crisis, not everything is drama, and not everything needs to be handled immediately or harshly.

- "That Falling Sky is Not Falling on Me!" This is the opposite of making things enlarged and fearsome. We take issues we should be concerned about (such as dating someone who has a drug issue, is involved in criminal activity, or treats us poorly) and shrink them down by explaining and rationalizing them away. This allows us to lull ourselves into the false belief that everything is fine, and swat away major issues like gnats on a summer day. But in fact, we're silencing critical alarm bells in our head because of the headache they cause.

- "I Am the Sun and The World Follows My Orbit": News flash—the world doesn't revolve around you! Yes, people's thoughts, days, and lives do not rise and set around your feelings, thoughts, or rigid agenda. That is a good thing—imagine the pressure if everyone's focus and dependence rested solely on you. Yet, some of us question and personalize everything. "Why did they do that to me? Why didn't they invite me? Why did I cause that to happen to them?"

It is not all about you, because you are simply not always in the forefront of *everyone's* mind. In fact, most issues occur simply because people _neglect_ to take the considerations and feelings of others into account (notice I said "neglect to," not "intend not to"). Knowing you are not on the center of the world's stage with everyone aiming a critical eye at you takes the pressure off... right?

- "The World and Others Control Me": You are ultimately in control of you. No-one can truly make you do, or not do, anything. The childhood excuse of "he/she made me do it" does not work as you mature. You cannot control the happiness or emotions of anyone else, nor can they control you. You can be neither the martyr nor the victim if you do not choose to be, or if you realize you are in control of yourself.

- "Life Should Be Fair": Do not expect life to be fair, and you will be much happier. If you expect fairness in life always, you will be disappointed constantly and beat your head against the proverbial wall of life (for more, see the "pile" on fairness).

- "Pointing the Finger at Others": As the adage goes, "When you point your finger at someone else, there are three others pointing back at you." Blaming others for your misgivings or failures does not serve to help you grow. Blaming takes the ball out of your court and puts it in someone else's hands, outside your control. Rather, ask yourself, "What are the areas for which I am responsible, and how can I change those?"

- "The "Shoulds," "Musts," "Have-tos": When you set rigid guidelines for yourself and your life, you will encounter a great deal of frustration and disappointment in yourself when you do not live up to the bar you set. We then beat ourselves with the belt of guilt for our failure. Conversely, when others don't live up to those "rules" we have falsely created, we attack them for not meeting our own expectations.

- "Trying to Get Others to Fit Into Our Shoes": Dr. Phillippa Lally, a psychologist and researcher at University College London, published a study in the *European Journal of Social Psychology* and found, "on average, it takes 66 days for a new habit to be instilled into a person."[5] Therefore, unless you have the time and energy to keep harping on someone each day, every day, for the next two months plus, stop trying. Accept people for who they are, and let them accept you at face value, as well. Trying to get someone to change involuntarily is like trying to shove your foot into a too-small shoe—you may end

---

[5] Lally, Phillippa, and Benjamin Gardner. "Promoting Habit Formation." *Health Psychology Review*, vol. 7, no. sup1, 2013, doi:10.1080/17437199.2011.603640.

up bloodying and blistering your foot, but in the end, the size of the shoe does not magically conform (unless your name is Cinderella).

- "Use Labels for Jars and Not People:" How many times do you call people by labels, such as "jerk", "bit*h", or worse? The problem with these labels is that your concept of "jerk" is different from my notion of "jerk." Your definition of a "loser" is different from mine. Once we label someone, how does it help us to change the issue? It does not—it only serves to make that person an object of anger and contempt, not a person worthy of resolving an issue or problem in a productive fashion between two persons who are equals.

- "Know-It-All": When you are right in an argument, it still does not help resolve the animosity one may feel when the conflict is more emotional than logical. Don't always try to be "right" or a "know-it-all". You will learn more and be far more effective in your relationships if you realize you don't know everything and that it is better to be happy with each other always than be "right" once. Who knows? Maybe you will learn something, as well.

- "If I Am a Martyr, I Will Get Something Out of It": This we also touched on earlier. Stop giving to get. That is to say, if you are "giving" to invest in the hope of a later payment with interest, you are merely exchanging, and not truly giving. If you really want to give altruistically, do so without any thought of getting anything back. If you do get something back, it will be a *happier* bonus—just don't expect it.

Pile #7
All Work and No Hobbies Makes You a Boring Boy/Gal

Our world can quickly become unbalanced. We are driven by many competing forces that encourage us to stretch ourselves in many directions for many different people. It leads one to wonder, what are we doing? If we are working, carpooling, eating, and sleeping, where does that leave time for a life?

It is necessary to think about that you are an important individual and adult outside the realm of your family and vocational obligations. Therefore, you must foster a life that fulfills you to allow you to give what you have left in your cup to others without any resentment or expectation of what's in it for you.

Find a hobby, at least one. It is necessary for you to have something to talk about (aside from your family or work), to build a skill, and to recreate yourself as a more well-rounded, *happier* individual. You are a person as well as a mother, father, husband, wife, daughter, or son. It is important that we feed and acknowledge all these roles, as well as that which encompasses the individual that is you.

Pile #8
Not Being Your Own Best Friend

When I work with young children, I always end our discussions with, "When you're sad or when you're blue... my best friend is me, and your best friend is you." The reason that this lesson is repeated *ad nauseam* is because it is so vital and ageless.

Often, we show a superficial kindness to those we meet on the street and to whom we have no connection. We frequently save our most bitter and biting dialogue for those we love most. Yet, there is one exception to that—we reserve the VERY harshest and most biting words for ourselves. We say things in our own internal dialogue that we would *NEVER* say to another human being. In doing so, we whip ourselves into a state of decreased self-esteem and increased self-loathing.

If you do only *one* thing for yourself, keep the words you tell yourself inside your mind *AT LEAST* as kind as any you would say to your friend. After all, relationships and friendships come and go, but you are stuck with you—make the best of it!

Pile #9
Overthinking Your Thoughts

By overthinking, we can make the best of scenarios a wreck within our own heads. We churn thoughts in an endless cycle like a laundry dryer, until we are left with a lot of lint and a few badly shrunk sweaters. The happiest of thoughts can have microscopic cracks if you look hard enough.

Stop overthinking—you can pick anything apart with constant questioning. Nothing is ever 100% certain or flawless, but when you focus on every minute detail, you can and will find flaws in anything and everything. Nothing, and I mean nothing, is perfect, but many things are great. However, this is not to say that you should be naive with challenges, either (more on that later).

Pile #10
Not Following the "Can You Put Your Head on the Pillow at Night" Test

In the quiet of the night is when many of our thoughts from throughout the day pour into our heads like a rainstorm. They disrupt our sleep and leave us tossing and turning, questioning our day and our choices, both large and small.

First off, those thoughts need to be freed. Like a shaken bottle of soda bubbling with the pressure of carbonation, eventually, the carbon dioxide needs to be released or it will continue to build until it explodes on everything around you like a fountain. Keeping a pen and journal next to you and writing down the thoughts (no matter how small or crazy you perceive them to be) helps release that pressure. It should be done "from brain to pen" because only then can they be released and fully examined on paper.

Next, when you are making choices throughout the day, ask yourself, "Can I put my head on the pillow at night over this decision?" In other words, "Does this choice align with my personal values and ethics? Or am I doing this because I am told to do it or out of blind allegiance to someone—or something—else?" Remember, it is generally better to hold steadfast than to go against your own principles, beliefs, and character. Those who "just follow orders" are often the ones swept into crises and lumped together with those whose course of action may not be consistent with your ethical beliefs when "push comes to shove."

Pile #11
Attempting to Win Best Actor/Actress in a Dramatic Series

We all know people like this. They are dramatic, and their drama leaves people scrambling around them. It could be the person who makes everything a crisis and acts as though the sky is falling down around them, the one who is easily offended by everyone and everything, or one who is a perpetual victim to the world around them.

As a child, you likely believed the world revolved around you—that is developmentally appropriate in childhood. This is why when a divorce occurs, family therapists advise that great care and time be dedicated to assuring the children that the divorce is not "their fault." Kids are predominantly egocentric and falsely believe that the divorce is due to something they did, or did not do, or maybe should have done differently.

They theorize with their limited life experience that the world revolves around their actions.

As you grow and mature, you should recognize that the world is no longer about you. In fact, the unfortunate truth is most people spend their time *not* thinking about you. Yes, even family and friends don't always center their lives around your wants or needs. So, when you use drama and tantrums, you show a clear lack of maturity to jar others into making you the center of attention again. Eventually people grow tired of exerting that much energy and time in a relationship. You become like the Boy (or Gal) Who Cried Wolf. People tire quickly of hearing about the "wolf" that may be around the corner, and when you do need them, they are simply too exhausted or frustrated to help when you truly are at your most vulnerable.

Pile #12
Thinking Common Sense Is Common

Here is a surprise for you—most people lack common sense. Yes, some of the things you hear now are common sense, but we all sometimes minimize our common sense, let emotions take the best of us, or just ignore the fact that there are practical rules and laws in life because they are not convenient to our current situation(s).

Pile #13
Logic Is Not Emotion and Vice Versa

Remember, emotions are not logical. So, when you try to be logical with emotions, just know they are not always there to make sense or be compatible partners with each other. In fact, emotions are often the opposite of "making sense." You cannot reason with emotions (yours or others). They just are, and we must try to get to the core of why we feel the way we do.

We also are quick to discount the emotions of others by saying, "You shouldn't feel that way." Again, emotions are not things that operate within the world of logic. We cannot shoo away another's emotions because, again, feelings/emotions "just are" and exist within the world of being human. Accept yours and those of others at face value. If you try to rationalize someone's emotions, just remember you are speaking two contradictory languages.

Pile #14
Being a Nice Guy/Gal and Believing You Always Finish Last

The old adage, "Nice guys finish last," has been around probably since the dawn of time. That nice caveman who let everyone eat before him would slowly starve to death. In modern society, the person who lets everyone climb the rungs of the promotional ladder ahead of him/her, as he/she holds it steady, may find themselves looking at the backsides of their former co-workers (and now their superiors) on that same ladder and having their head stepped on over and over.

It should be noted, however, that if you want to be happy, niceness should not be equated with weakness. "Nice" and "strong" are not polar opposites. In our world, we have people who live along a spectrum of extreme passivity to extreme aggression. Yes, the aggressive ones may succeed at first, but the fiery anger with which they burn often leads them to trouble with others or society as a whole. These people may reach the top, but they may not last there because they have done it on the bruised backs of those they have climbed over along the way. In short, their impulsive and volatile natures make them their own worst enemies.

Then there are those who are passive. They teach everyone around them that their name should be "Matt" because they can be walked over, and people can (and will) wipe their feet on them. These people "bottle everything up" and regret not saying how they feel or what they wish they could say because they're terrified that others won't like them. Instead, they turn that anger inward and become saddened and crappy, and then feel helpless and hopeless.

Being nice doesn't mean that you cannot express yourself or establish your beliefs or boundaries firmly. If you worry about hurting someone else's feelings, you likely don't have to worry because being overly harsh is not innate in your personality. What you do have to worry about when you feel strongly regarding something is not voicing it. When you say it, say why you feel that way and offer a solution to the problem. Be kind, but be firm.

If you do not say what you want to say, you will find it coming out somewhere else when it is not effective. You will become resentful or burnt out, or you may explode about your aggressive supervisor in a tirade against your innocent loved ones at home. You may harbor angry feelings inside the recesses of your mind and let them stew and ferment. None of these things are remotely conducive to that "nice" persona you hope to embody in others' eyes.

Pile #15
Staying Down

This is going to sound like New Age or inspirational mumbo jumbo, but the only way you fail is by giving up. You may say, "Yeah, but I've tried that ten times and failed." Yes, but have you learned anything? You've "tried and failed," but did you gain anything?

I'll give you a "for instance"—I tried for seven years to climb the ladder in my own profession. For seven years, I built up my resumé, did everything I could to shore up my weaknesses and bolster my strengths. It led to a frustrating road, taking me nowhere near where I thought I wanted to go. I contemplated to myself, "I failed... After seven years, I finally give up."

What I forgot was that it is not about reaching the ultimate goal—rather, it is about the journey. In that time of striving, I received many awards, had many new experiences, was offered many professional opportunities (that I may not have had otherwise), and began writing (initially to prove myself worthy for the job). What it did lead to was teaching at the postgraduate level, writing articles (that eventually led to invitations to write books), and increased time with my family. The journey of life was the goal, not the initial destination I thought I sought.

However, if I had given up at any point, these goals would have never made themselves evident. Regardless of whether you meet the goal you had in mind, it is the trying that is crucial. You never know where it will take you (unless you quit at it prematurely).

Pile #16
Firing Before You Aim

If I were to say, "Ready... aim..." your next word would likely be, "Fire!" The reason we follow this sequence is that we must be ready when we are making a big decision—we must aim toward that decision, and then take decisive action.

Some of us, however, have the sequence confused. We "fire" first out of excitement or impulse, and then we try to figure out what to do from there. Problem is, you can't put the bullet (or decision) back into the gun—it is too late. Or we "aim" and "fire" but are not "ready" (for the potential consequences or fallout). This occurs when we are not fully prepared for the consequences of our actions because we have not been proactive in our judgment(s). This may occur when you are not "ready" for a relationship or job but "aim and fire" anyway because you wanted it and it dropped into your lap at the wrong time.

Pile #17
Always Being Offended

As the internet speeds communication to frenetic and ever more simplified levels, it seems most everyone is in a perpetual state of being chronically "offended." They are offended at each other's thoughts, offended that they were not told something, offended at another's beliefs, offended that they were not invited somewhere, offended that they were not offended, etc.

It is so easy to get drawn into this negativity, but first off, most people are not on a mission to personally offend you. It becomes offensive when you take it personally.

Secondly, when you set out from the vantage point established by the words, "I am easily offended," guess what? You will always be easily offended. Everything becomes a battle wherein you stand on the defensive when there is nothing that needs to be defended. People will not mysteriously see the light and change their course because little ol' you is offended. It often becomes a waste of energy that could be better harnessed for some other vital part of your life.

Do not set your expectations on the lofty framework of what you believe you should expect from others, or become offended when they do not follow the path you thought, or to the degree you wanted. Consider as well how your history influences your current sensitivity.

Pile #18
Doing the Same and Expecting Different

The greatest genius of the 20th century, Albert Einstein, is credited with the following quote: "Insanity: doing the same thing over and over again and expecting different results." Though it is doubtful that Einstein was the first to say this, it is nevertheless an important element of happiness. Most of us use the limited tools in our toolbox to try to solve a problem. When we can't solve it, we tend to work harder and more aggressively out of frustration, using the same tired old strategies, versus trying something different. As psychologist Albert Maslow warned, "If all you have is a hammer, everything looks like a nail."

Hence, if all you have in your toolbox is a proverbial hammer, you will try that tool repeatedly and get the same result. If you are using the same old strategies in your relationships, at your job, in searching for what you want, consider a different strategy and see if perhaps it fosters a different result.

What is the different strategy? That depends on the situation.

Ask yourself these questions:
- Be honest with yourself—why is this strategy not working?
- Are you not seeing something?
- Is this something you really want? Are you sabotaging yourself out of fear?
- What are the subtle elements in this issue that you may not be seeing clearly?
- Are you being too critical of yourself and others?
- Are you lying or manipulating yourself to find the easiest way out?

Pile #19
Not Claiming Your Baggage

We all have baggage in our lives. Whether it be a difficult childhood, a challenging health or emotional issue, or a past tumultuous relationship, you must come to peace with it. Claim it as yours, admit it, accept it, forgive it, and move on. We often try to push these things to the back of our heads, run from them, or make excuses for their holding us back from our lives.

Running from them is like trying to outrun a lion—you may be able to run for a little while, but it will overtake you at some point much sooner than later. Making excuses for your baggage does not allow you to learn from it or take pride in what you have overcome. Feeling sorry for yourself leaves you in the same position as when you were victimized, and stunts the growth that can come from a difficult time or position.

Pile #20
Using Drinking, Drugs, Food, or Sex to Forget About Your Crappiness

Often, when we are in the darkest of moods, we look for a short-term relief as a "pick-me-up" from the dank cellar of our own emotional demons. The issue is that what we often inadvertently dig ourselves a deeper hole.

When a lifeguard goes out to make a rescue in the ocean, the greatest danger is rarely the rip current, sharks, or waves crashing around them—it is the very person they are rescuing. That hapless drowner will pull their prospective rescuer down to the bottom of the ocean to gain just a single breath of air. True, it may be their final gasp, and if they simply cooperated they would be brought to land and take many breaths for the rest of their lives. But they don't care about the long-term—they want a breath, and they want it now. Their frantic thought is, "The heck with the next breaths—I want relief *now*."

If you have a drug, drinking, or another addictive issue, recognize it and get immediate professional help. You cannot find happiness if you are drowning and looking for your next gasp of air for a momentary and fleeting escape. I repeat, get help and get it now. Your life and happiness are waiting.

Pile #21
Having to be Right

On court shows, the attorneys attempt to show that they are right by giving a list of arguments that support their case. They do it in a manner that is sometimes passionate, often logical, but frequently convincing.

When we were children, we hated being wrong—for example, on a test that was returned with a big red F at the top. Subsequently, you had to explain your mistakes to your parents. You were ashamed and felt that you were licking your wounds with your tail between your legs. In tests, there are right and wrong answers, as well as good and bad consequences.

In life, it is not that simple. Trying to prove you are "right" in an emotional interaction does little for the connection between you and the other person—rather, it tears down the self-confidence or emotional integrity of someone you care about. Being "right" and "winning" in a relationship are often two very different things.

If you want to be happier, seek to solve the problem jointly, as opposed to proving why you were right and defeating the other person's ability to save face.

Doing so fosters a relationship of caring, safety, and support.

Pile #22
Letting Lists/Chores/Responsibilities Govern Your Daily Life

How many of us love our lists? We have lists on sticky notes, lists on refrigerators, lists on smartphones, and lists on lists. These lists govern and drive our very existence.

Several years ago, there was a popular video game called Tetris. The object was simple—fit the puzzle pieces neatly together on the bottom as they fall faster and faster from atop the screen. As you fitted each piece, it would disappear only to have an infinite number of other pieces fall from the top. Eventually, the screen filled, and you ultimately lost as a stack of video puzzle pieces filled the screen.

Lists are like this videogame of yesteryear—responsibilities keep coming at an endless clip and we try to fit all of them together. If you are not careful, the lists master you and you are enslaved by them. They can easily push out all that *happier* stuff like recreation, rest, and time with friends and family. The mundane cleaning, working, and carpools are always there, but they don't create many memories to treasure, do they?

To take control of your lists and make them *happier*, consider the following ideas:

- Do First Things First: The things you don't want to do will be the greatest source of procrastination. Get them done first, and the rest will be downhill from there.
- Prioritize: Not everything on your list is as important as everything else. Not everything is equally time-sensitive, either. Make note of this in your lists by prioritizing.
- Structure Lists by Time, Not by Completion: If you make lists, one thing that's for sure is that they multiply. Like rabbits, one task becomes two, and two become two hundred. If you measure success by completing a daily list, you will always find the list defeating you. Measuring your lists by time instead, that is, "I will do everything to complete what is on my list until 2:00 pm. At 2:00, the rest of the list is

deferred until tomorrow. Therefore, I have the rest of the day to do something of my own choosing."

- Include Time for Yourself on Your List: If you do not slate in time for yourself on your list, it will not happen. Lists of "what you have to do for everyone else" quickly crowd out time for yourself. Slate out a time for you, time with your significant other, and time for your family/friends. Most days should include a little play, as well, to balance things out for a happier versus crappier life.

Pile #23
Living in the Past... Living in the Future

It is so easy to remember the past and dwell there. The problem is that we often distort the past and make it appear better than it may have truly been. After all, they don't call them "the bad ol' days," right?

Memories are wonderful—however, they have a way of fermenting over the years like a sweetening wine. Old memories can be distorted in a positive way or not fully appreciated when they are seen through the lens of the present.

Not only are our past thoughts not quite accurate, but they are not a place in which we can live forever. If you spend time always looking in the rearview mirror of life, you miss the scenery directly in front of you.

To stay present-focused:
- Recognize that worry is past- or future-focused: If you hear "what if" in your head, you are veering off the road of remaining present. If you are always using the past tense, you are living life looking behind you.
- Use visualization or meditation: Using these age-old techniques can teach you to appreciate and focus on the minute details of the now.
- Don't complicate your life: Handle only what is on your plate right now, not what you had on your plate or what you want next on it.

Pile #24
Being Too Proud to Ask for Help

In the previous "piles" we discussed how we try to hide the imperfections of our lives and put our best face forward to project what we hope society may desire. Often that mask of a "fake smile" can become exhausting. Our muscles become achy and tired as we try to maintain an act and a smile that are not genuine.

We carry that empty smile wherever we go. When someone asks, "How are you doing?" you answer with a simple and empty, "Good... How 'bout you?" So, your life continues, in which you hide the sadness inside and allow those demons to fester and metastasize like a shameful cancer. It may surprise you to find that in other cultures, that same question is answered honestly, and the respondent will say if they are doing lousy and in need of help. In other cultures, it is a question, not merely a formality.

If you need help, get it. Don't wait on it another minute—we are placed on this earth to all help each other. If you need your car fixed, you go to a mechanic. If you want your macchiato, you go to a barista. If physically ill, you go to your medical doctor—there is no shame in that. If you need help, it is your job and duty to be fair to yourself and family by finding out what you need.

Pile #25
Blaming Everyone Else

Do you ever notice when you are on the roads that you tend to become frustrated with those slower than you—whom you classify as "the idiots"—while those driving faster are harshly labeled "the maniacs"? Now, you may have far more colorful language for these people and may even do your fair share of using "the bird" to communicate with those drivers. However, ask yourself this—if you fail to follow every posted road sign exactly at all times, what makes you qualified to critique all those around you?

There is a term in psychology called "attribution bias", or "attributional bias", which refers to a slanting of one's thinking and to the systematic errors made when people evaluate or try to find reasons for their own and others' behaviors.[6] In short, it means we tend to believe that if someone is not doing something exactly as we do, they are doing it

---

[6] Stangor, Dr. Charles. "Principles of Social Psychology – 1st International Edition." *Biases in Attribution | Principles of Social Psychology – 1st International Edition*, 26 Sept. 2014, opentextbc.ca/socialpsychology/chapter/biases-in-attribution/.

wrong and therefore are subject to having our fingers figuratively pointed in their faces.

The issue then becomes that when you blame someone else for something, you don't learn how to change things for yourself in a positive manner. If everything is someone else's fault, you are absolved of all guilt, power, or control. What is worse than not having control of a situation where you may be able to change for the good in your own life?

As the saying goes, "When you point a finger at someone else, three are pointing back at you." Therefore, instead of using the words "they, he, she, you", use the word "I". What can "I" do to change the situation? What did "I" do to contribute to the problem? What do "I" want to do next? "I" is a far more effective means of change than "you," "them," "they," or "but".

Pile #26
Needing to Be in Control of Everything

It is great to be in control of everything. If you could have total control, you would know what is over the horizon, what is around every corner or turn, and adjust accordingly. Unfortunately, it only takes one look at the weather forecasters to know we are not in control or knowledgeable about every aspect of this unpredictable game called life.

Some of us cannot grasp that concept, and so we try to find ways of "controlling" by "white-knuckling" our way through life like someone who hates thrill rides, grasping the seatbelt of a rollercoaster and screaming and cursing at every turn, drop, and upside-down loop.

Focusing on what you can control versus obsessing over what you can't control will help you step over this "pile" and work toward your happiness.

You Generally Can Control:
- How *you* respond to someone.
- The choices *you* make.
- How *you* handle your emotions.
- How *you* care for your emotional, physical, and spiritual health.
- How and with whom *you* spend your leisure time.
- *Your* priorities.
- What *you* are grateful for.

You Cannot Control:

- The choices *others* make.
- How *others* respond to you.
- Changing *others* to be the way you "want" them to be or motivating them accordingly.
- The politics of *the world* and the uncertain nature of life.

Pile #27
Not Following Your Priorities

It is important to have priorities. If you establish none, then nothing is a priority, or the ones you have shift chaotically like the plates of the Earth creating an earthquake that causes everything to fall down around you.

Do you know someone who is overly dramatic about everything? For them, everything is a big deal and/or a crisis. The problem becomes that if they categorize everything as urgent, then nothing is urgent. How do you make an emergency more of an emergency? Put another way, if everything is a priority, then nothing is a priority, and everything is up for grabs in your world.

So, ask yourself—what are my priorities?
Are they:
1. Family?
2. Work?
3. Friends?
4. Hobbies?
5. Other?

In what order do you see these in your life? As the rains of life's pressures pour down over us, having priorities can be the umbrella to avoid becoming soaked and inundated with the question of, "What should I do?" Furthermore, stressors cause us great emotional confusion and anxiety if we don't know in advance what is most vital in our lives, because we don't know in what order to handle competing responsibilities.

If your family is most important, you may have to sacrifice other things at times to make room for them. If work is most important, then you may be need to forego hobbies or other obligations when they interfere with your career.

A key to happiness lies within knowing that you can have *anything* you want—you just can't have *everything* you want whenever you want it. Deciding which things you want and holding steadfast to that plan cuts down on the stalling/procrastinating of not knowing what to do and when to do it.

Pile #28
Thinking Comfort Is Always Best

Some of us stay in bad situations because they are predictable. There is a certain comfort in knowing what is coming down the pike. Predictability brings with it the belief, "Well, I know what I have... I don't know what I am going to get." Yes, but does knowing what you will get every day lead to happiness? If what you are getting is simply more of the same mediocre satisfaction, and you are in an emotional purgatory, is it worth mere comfort?

Lack of comfort can also be exhilarating—it can be the change of pace needed to make things better. When you make a simple adjustment from an endless cycle of doing the same things repeatedly, it is like changing one cog in a machine. Each part of the machine is systematically affected by the seemingly minute alterations. That one positive shift may lead to changes that you never thought would take you to a new world and opportunities down the road.

Pile #29
Making Life More Complicated Than It Needs to Be

Sometimes the best answer is also the simplest and most obvious answer. Overthinking the simple makes it complicated and leads to confusion. If you find yourself making a big deal over the tiniest and simplest of issues, it may be time to bring it back down to the "K.I.S.S." principle you may have heard when doing math in middle school: "Keep It Simple, Stupid."

Keep simple things simple. Plenty of things are complicated in life, but not everything has to be complicated, or made more so by your actions.

Pile #30
Trying to be Something You Are Not

Remember high school, that uncertain time when you stood in the dressing room of life? We all tried to decide if we "fit" into the various molds and lifestyles set by our peers. We each tried to see if we wanted to be a jock, a musician, a loner, an academic.

With each of these we experimented with elements of who we might be, or think we want to be. We see if one type fits better than another, with the hope that we will find ourselves and fit in with the right social group and the society of peers we hope to join. For many teens, this is an incredibly painful time as they realize that they are not a single "type" but an amalgamation of some (or many) types that often blend together in adulthood. Until then, they find the growing pains of figuring out themselves by feeling their way through adolescent life.

I say this because some of us never get fully out of that stage, and remain in a perpetual state of uncertain *crappiness*. As an adult, hopefully you have come to terms with who you are. Not everyone likes who you are. You do not have the same interests as everyone, and so inevitably stop trying to be something you are not. Furthermore, you might try to be overly extroverted when that is not what you enjoy.

Don't be the partier, if you would rather be a homebody. Yes, you should push yourself out of your comfort zone, as it is good to avoid becoming trapped within yourself. However, beating yourself up for failing to be something you are not holds you back from recognizing the strengths of everything you ***ARE***!

Pile #31
Believing You Should Be the Life of the Party or Very Extroverted

In our Western Society, popular belief says that everyone should strive for independence and be the outgoing life of the party. Our world seeks to be competitive, and breeds people who are fiercely individualistic and can handle the world like a cowboy handles the dusty and rugged world of the Wild, Wild West.

This contrasts greatly with Eastern Society, which says one should listen and learn, versus talking and expressing themselves constantly and in a perpetually animated fashion. Eastern society encourages people to collaborate as a system, rather than as individuals (and not take the glory of achievement solely for themselves), and to seek quiet time for solace and reflection as a means of self-improvement versus networking and socializing.

The point is this—stop thinking that because you don't fall into the category of people who seek, or are always able, to be witty and carry on lengthy conversations, you should beat yourself up and feel *crappy*. Understand that those who are introverted can be leaders and rise to the top of their fields. In fact, a study conducted in 2012 by researchers at University of Pennsylvania found that introverted leaders are often able to deliver better results, because "instead of promoting the loudest, flashiest initiatives, they're more likely to let talented colleagues run with good ideas." [7] In short, they bring out the best in others without needing to steal the spotlight for themselves.

Those with a slant toward introversion also realize that relationships are not about quantity—they are about quality. Introverted people are cautious in establishing friendships, but when they do, they are strong and long-lasting. Additionally, introverted people tend to be cautious and avoid making rash, impulsive moves. In their self-reflection, they don't tend to make moves that can lead to stepping into other piles of *crappiness*. Additionally, because of this reflectiveness, they will go against the grain of simply following orders or just trying to make everyone happy.

Pile #32
Wanting to Be More Introverted Because You Are Extroverted

Again, don't change who you are. Every personality type has strengths and weaknesses. If I am too assertive, one might say I am aggressive. If I am too passive, I am a doormat. Too kind? "Who needs someone to always be so happy? There must be something they are hiding." Too strong, "That person is a jerk, b*tch, etc."

The point is, you *WILL NOT* make everyone happy, so you might as well make yourself and those closest to you happy, right? Do you care what the annoying co-worker or person you meet on the street thinks more than those who are closest to your heart? I would hope not.

Pile #33
Expecting that Changing Your Outside Will Change the Inside

Many of us diet and exercise—some even undergo radical plastic surgery in hopes of changing our bodies. However, no matter how much you change the outside, your inside remains the same.

In one of my previous books, I discussed how many of us look at the body of a car. If it looks sleek and new, we assume that what's under the hood must be just as pristine, until we take it to a mechanic who says the engine is blown, the gaskets are worn, or the battery is dead. In short, I would not buy this car if it were the last car on the lot.

The same applies to changing your appearance. It may help to bolster your self-esteem and happiness in the short-term, but the harder work of dealing with your own internal baggage and insecurities is the most vital element in making long-lasting change.

Gravity and age will one day have their way with you. You will have less hair in the places you want it, and more in those areas you don't. Your body will wrinkle and sag, and your belly may well overlap your belt. What will you have left? Your own self-esteem, the dialogue you have with yourself, and relationships with others.

Pile #34
Not Having a Religious or Spiritual Center to Your Life

This is not a book on spirituality or religion. There are volumes of materials that intertwine religion, spirituality, and mental health as well as counseling, and I would encourage you to read them, dependent on your religious and spiritual leaning. These publications provide a strong framework of purpose and a "centered life" for many.

However, it should be noted that many scientific studies do, in fact, correlate spirituality and/or religion to happiness. Take the case of a 2015 study conducted by economic and medical researchers at the London School of Economics and the Erasmus University Medical Center in the Netherlands, who determined that regular participation in some religious activity was the *only* type of event that led to consistent and prolonged happiness.[7] This provided an even greater positive emotional boost than other activities usually correlated with life satisfaction such as volunteering, returning to school, or even being an active member in community-based organizations.

Pile #35
"If I Only Had More Money, I Would Be Happier and Less Crappy."

So, how much money do you need to be happy?

If you made $10,000 more a year, would you be ten times happier? If you won one hundred million dollars in the lottery, would that translate into you

---

[7] "Does Spirituality Make You Happy?" *Time*, Time, time.com/4856978/spirituality-religion-happiness/.

being one hundred million times happier? These comparisons may seem ridiculous, but there is likely not a specific number or income that would make you happiest. If you reach a certain number, "buyer's remorse" always says, "Yeah, but I want a little more… so I can buy a little bigger house, a little better car, etc."

In 2011, Princeton researchers made headlines with a new study showing that happiness increases along with income up until $75,000, after which point it plateaus.[8] The bigger house, the nicer car? They only provide short-term happiness. If they result in working twenty-four hours a day, look at the cost versus value analysis. In short, is the time and effort worth the materialistic outcome generated?

Pile #36
Discarding Ways to Relieve Anxiety Without Fully Researching or Understanding Them

When some people hear words like meditation and visualization, they shy away. Their "visualization"

---

[8] Rubin, Courtney. "At What Price Happiness? $75,000." *Inc.com*, Inc., www.inc.com/news/articles/2010/09/study-says-$75,000-can-buy-happiness.html.

concept is some New Age, white-bearded man with a long, flowing robe talking about crystals and how astrology and tea leaves can read the future. For some, this is a huge turn-off, and so they turn away to find alternate ways of lessening the *crappiness* of anxiety.

However, these techniques have been used for thousands of years in Eastern (and other) cultures with great success. Just employing some of the techniques of meditation and visualization can help take your "*crappy*" time and begin to shift the tides to a "*happier*" day.

1. Find a quiet place in your home or wherever you are. It is important that all of us have a place to find peace and quiet, to find and center ourselves. If you would like to boost this experience and "tune out "stressors, find something that makes "white noise" or use relaxing music.
2. Sit in a comfortable position.
3. Close your eyes, and slowly take deep breaths. Concentrate solely on your breathing. If you have thoughts of what you are going to do, what you have done, or the whirling of thoughts in your head, listen to them without judgment as though you are detached and

watching a television show of your life detailing these thoughts. Try to bring your reflections, however, back to your inhaling and exhaling.

4. Slowly open your eyes and ease yourself back into your daily routine.

Basic Guided Imagery (slight modification of the above strategy):

1. Find a quiet place where you will not be disturbed and can focus.
2. Close your eyes and imagine your favorite place or vacation for relaxation.
3. Think about what you would see, smell, hear, and feel in this place. Concentrate on every minute detail of these sights, sounds, and senses until you can look around and imagine being there.
4. Take deep, relaxing breaths as you go from where you are to the imaginary place where you want to be.
5. Slowly open your eyes and ease yourself back into your daily routine.

Pile #37
Not Having a GPS for Your Life

Some of us become frustrated because we have stalled in some aspect of the business of life. We simply lack direction and an aptitude for turning on our internal GPS. In turn, we wander around making the same mistakes again and again. When the next year passes, the next five years pass, or a decade, we find ourselves circling the roundabout of life, and are tired, frustrated, and crapped out.

Let's take another tactic—if I had a GPS in my car and wanted to get somewhere, I would program the GPS to take me my chosen destination. That's common sense, right? Well, think about the GPS of your life—do you know where you are programming it to go?

Let me ask this a different way. If, at the end of your long and healthy life, someone was to write an obituary on you, what would it say? A better question might be, what would you WANT it to say? That is the difference between driving with your life GPS unprogrammed and programming it for a life of meaning and destination.

Ask yourself as you program your life GPS:

- What would you ideally want people to say as a brother, sister, parent, husband/wife?
- What would you ideally want your friends to say about you?
- When someone talks about your life achievements, what would you want those to be?
- If someone were to describe you, how would they do it?
- When they talk about your strengths, how would those be conveyed to others?
- What would you like your legacy to be?

Pile #38
Waiting Outside the Room and Not Going In

Some of us spend our time waiting and trying to figure out what we want to do in several domains within our lives. We wait for a definitive indication as to what we should do, or some kind of abstract "sign". When that does not arrive, we are left in a *crappy* purgatory, in-between doing something and doing nothing. You can only ask so many friends, family, and professionals for advice. Then you are left to make a choice—the key is to make an educated and good decision. Either way, you will feel better when you tried than you would if you stalled out and waited too long.

Pile #39
Believing That Crappiness is Permanent

Not to wax philosophical, but nothing is permanent—not your career, not your relationships, not your life. Sound negative?

Not necessarily—this means that when you are on a high or a low of life, you must remember it is not permanent. If you are having a crappy time, the storm clouds will clear. If it is a happy time, that too (unfortunately) will flatten out eventually.

Many of us are programmed to give heavy credence to the negative and, in turn, never fully realize or appreciate the positive. Many in counseling informally call that the "5:1 Rule". That is, it will take five positive statements to gloss over one harsh remark that was uttered by another (perhaps) thoughtlessly or without a filter.

Pile #40
When Tragedy Occurs... How Do You Make Any **Crappiness** *Into* **Happiness**?

The short answer is that when tragedy, grief, and loss enter your life, you cannot turn those into happiness. It is appropriate for you to grieve, cry, and embrace the full spectrum of feelings that may sweep across your emotional landscape. Many people believe that there is a "right way" to deal with loss and grief. There is generally not—everyone deals with sadness in their own way and, despite many books, there is no official "manual" for how to deal with these issues.

That being said, you must maintain your mental health. In the case of loss, it is your duty after you mourn to decide how to carry on the legacy and wishes of those who are no longer with you on Earth. This means balancing your sadness with the happiness of their memories that they would want you to cherish, as well. How can you carry on their memory in a positive way?

This can be done by helping to care for those in their life, helping a worthy cause, or volunteering. In short, keep their memories and wishes alive. That is your duty, and in performing it, you bring forward the best of what that person could no longer do here on Earth and cherish their memory even further, as well as their legacy.

Pile #41
Everyone Is Counting on Me ... I'm The ONLY One Who Could Do This or That

Wow! What an ego it takes to believe that you are the *ONLY* one who could do anything! For every person capable of doing anything, there are countless others who could do that task as well.

So, don't feel like you need to do everything. It is more of an ego trip than it is a realistic viewpoint. Delegate and recognize that you doing everything yourself indicates a lack of trust in others. If you delegate, you are working as a team, not a single person who feels it is their duty as a martyr who is always burning the midnight oil.

Pile #42
Keeping Yourself Too Busy to Breathe

In our world now, we try to pack as much into our lives as possible. If you are a parent, you also try to keep your children as occupied as possible in the hope that they will be well-balanced individuals.

In turn, everyone's life is ironically made more out of balance. Leisure and free time are necessary components to balance life. If you cannot breathe and rest, you cannot be balanced.

Pile #43
Not Wanting ANYONE to Judge You

Yes, it is true that some people will judge you based on your looks, money, politics, culture, etc. This is an unfortunate reality. Nevertheless, what will lead to sadness is if you try to constantly pursue these people and try to "convince" them to like you or have a change of heart.

It is better to spend your time bolstering relationships with people who accept you for you. Trying to be a chameleon or be something (or someone) you are not will lead you to be fake and artificial, and ultimately waste your time.

Pile #44
Believing You Can Be Good at Everything

We are all born with certain inherent strengths. Yes, you can hone and sharpen deficits—however, be aware that you cannot be the best at everything. Be at peace with the fact that you are not so good at some things. Be able to laugh at yourself in these cases. You cannot always take yourself so seriously.

Pile #45
Thinking Everything is a Big "Crappy" Issue

This is worthy of saying again—if everything is a big deal, nothing is a big deal. Do not waste emotion or energy on small issues such as:

1. The everyday comments others make that you feel you must dissect and figure out "what they meant."
2. The small mistakes you make every day.
3. Trying to discern the potential "alternate meanings" of email, texts, or social media posts.
4. Worrying about a person's opinion based on a superficial contact when you have very little connection with, need for, or interaction(s) with them.

Pile #46
Allowing Worry to Monopolize Your Happiness

According to the Anxiety and Depression Association of America (ADAA), anxiety/worry disorders are the most common mental issue in the U.S., which impacts approximately 40 million adults in the United States, age 18 and older. Put another way, worry and other forms of anxiety impact 18.1% of the population annually.[9] Others theorize that this figure may be even higher—however, many may just accept their extreme discomfort alone and in silence, or are afraid of potential stigma.

If you are a constant worrier, you rob some *happiness* from your life every day that you live out of sync with the present. It may not drain you totally of that elation, but it takes act like a colander, poking tiny holes in the enjoyment of your regular, day-to-day functioning.

To help alleviate some of your worry, consider the following:

1. Debate with your worries: Often when you think something, your brain immediately assumes what you ponder is true. Think about when you have an outrageous nightmare. You wake up in a cold sweat believing, in part, that it was real.

---

[9] "Facts & Statistics." *Anxiety and Depression Association of America, ADAA*, adaa.org/about-adaa/press-room/facts-statistics.

Similarly, when you think something, your brain is inclined to believe it as 100% true without question. It is similar to how, when you look at an optical illusion, you see what you see with 100% certainty (even though it can be viewed from a number of other perspectives that are technically all "100%" correct).

So, debate your thoughts. Ask, are these thoughts accurate? What are the statistics/chances that this could actually happen? Are you certain that you have all the facts? If it did happen, how would you handle it? What support would you have?

2. Recognize that when you have too many thoughts in your head: Often we believe that we have "too much in our head" and we become overwhelmed. In reality, when you look at your thoughts on paper, it is not hundreds or even a double-digit number of ideas or fears bulging out of your ears. Rather, it is often the same four or five thoughts that constantly run through your head like some horrid carousel. Recognizing this may help to tame that feeling of being overwhelmed.

3. Write down your thoughts straight from brain to pen: Writing down your thoughts EXACTLY as you hear them in your head when they occur can help you get them out of your head and onto paper, where you can meet them on neutral ground and battle with them fairly for a rational debate.

4. Recognize the "What-if-ers": Most worries in your head begin with the phrase, "What if?" When you hear these in your head, it should be a trigger in your thoughts, telling you, "I am about to worry."

5. Are you going to worry effectively? It is not that worrying is a bad thing. On the contrary, if you never worry, you will get yourself into impulsive and dangerous situations. That said, are you a good worrier? Are you able to find proactive and productive means of solving issues? If you are not, look toward others to help you.

6. Stay in the here and now: Worry is often elusive because it exists on the fringes of the future or the past. If you want to solve problems, focus only on the "here and now," and on what you can do to address the issue

immediately. Additionally, try techniques such as visualization and mindfulness (described earlier) that you can employ to keep present without worry or judgment.

6. Find a time to worry: Worrying can also be thought of as your brain growing undisciplined. There is a time for everything, and our brains tend to seek worry when they have idle time on their hands. If you think about it, you are not worrying "all the time." Rather, you are worrying during those quiet times (e.g. while working on something, getting ready to get up or go to sleep, or driving in the car). Worry comes like waves. Therefore, giving yourself a specific time to worry puts worrying in its place. When you do worry, however, do not allow yourself _not_ to worry during your designated "worry time"—instead, encourage yourself to find productive solutions.

8. Remind yourself of successes: Think about the last time you worried and experienced anticipation about something coming up. You worried more as you got closer to the point of doing it. Then you perhaps thought, "That wasn't so bad." You moved on to the next

worry without giving yourself credit for how well you handled the issue. Don't forget successes over your worries and fears—pat yourself on the back.

9. Worry is like The Wizard: Remember the Wizard of Oz? He had that holographic alien face, and flames billowing from the sides of the large gold towers that paralleled him. Dorothy and her party of friends were panicked and afraid. Then they realized that behind the curtain was a little elf of a man who also cowered in fear. Often worry is dressed like a wizard, but is actually a minute wisp of handling an actual event.

Pile #47
Plugging Your Ears and Not Listening to Those Around You

Have you ever seen a bratty child who puts their fingers in their ears and clamps their eyes shut when they do not want to hear or see something? It may be when their parent tries to enforce a consequence, or when a peer tells them something they simply don't want to hear.

We do that as adults, as well. Now, we may not plug our ears with our fingers or shut our eyes to the world outside, but we do something very similar—we filter out and ignore the information that we do not want to know.

It can be a warning about a potential mate, an upcoming issue, or the way you are acting. We "hear" it, all right, but we don't want to listen to it. We think it is too painful, too difficult to address, too honest and direct, and so we put it on the back shelf of our brain in a tightly sealed container, never to be heard or opened again. However, that very information may be what we need to access for our ultimate success or liberation from our own emotional prison. Listen to what is said before you discount anything—*truly* listen to see if it has any potential to help you assist yourself.

Pile #48
Not Wanting to be Alone

Just as it is good to jump out of your comfort zone to grow, it is also good to be alone with yourself at times. You cannot get to know yourself fully through the eyes of another. If you do not know yourself, how do you know what you want? In other words, if I know nothing about Georgian cuisine, then how do I know what I want to order? If you do not know yourself, you cannot know how to align yourself.

Pile #49
Feeling Sorry for Yourself

Feeling sorry for yourself is like keeping your head down and ignoring your surroundings as you walk. If you stare at the piles on the ground, you miss the things ahead. You also become selfish because you think, "Poor me," and lose the ability to see the need to contribute to others, empathize fully, or be a part of the world at large. It becomes a comfortable (though not pleasant) zone, as well as a blanket that will ultimately smother you as you feel validated without anyone else listening or contributing to your pity party.

Pile #50
Holding on to the Past and Fear of Change

Some of us constantly grip the world with white knuckles. We are trying to solve the riddle of life. "If I just do this, or just do that, things will be taken care of." The truth is that life is in a constant state of change. You will never "solve" the riddle—you are a manager of your life, and that means you can be proactive, but never will your life remain static. No change is equitable to going backward (or not living at all).

Pile #51
Believing that Someone Controls (Or Makes) You Do Something/Controls Your Emotions

When we were children, we would often point fingers at someone else and say they "made me do it." Alternatively, they "caused" me to feel that way. This is immature behavior, and it makes you powerless because you give control to someone else.

You can never control someone else's emotions or reactions to you. That said, you can always control how you react to someone. If someone is angry, and you mirror it, you escalate that emotion. If you display calm and patience, this says more about you and your maturity than it does about those around you. You *choose* what you do, or how to react—you are not "made" to do anything. As a child, you may have been "made" to do things that were out of your control—not so as an adult who can select what you want with relative autonomy.

Pile #52
Being Nearsighted

When you only look directly in front of you, you forget what is ahead. When this happens, you find yourself "putting out fires" and not dealing with the larger issues that take you off the treadmill of life and toward making productive, efficient progress in your life.

True, you should stay present and grounded to avoid anxiety and worrying about "what if" or staying grounded in the past. However, it is important to think efficiently by asking yourself, "Where do I want to go?" Instead of worrying and never getting anywhere, this allows you to guide your plans in an intentional direction.

Ask yourself:
- Where do you see yourself physically, emotionally, vocationally, socially, and financially in a month, a year, or five years?
- If you could do anything in work, travel, or socially, what would it look like? How do you get there?
- The more specificity, the better: Don't be vague. Use specific names, time frames, ideas, and words. The more obscure and

sketchy these details are, the harder it will be to focus on a goal.

- Not all items are equally important: As mentioned in this book repeatedly, you can get what you want—just not whatever you want, whenever you want it. Not all things are equally important, and if everything is as a priority, then nothing is. Order your goals so you know what you want more than anything else.

- Break things down to specifics: If you look at a five-year goal, it can (and should) appear overwhelming. After all, it is hard to do something in five years, or even in just one. If you break down items into "bite-sized" chunks for the next 3 months, 6 months, and a year, the plan will seem more doable.

- Review these often: Those 3-month, 6 month-, one-year, and three-year periods are good times to climb the tree of life, look down, and ask yourself, "Am I getting there?"

- Ask yourself why: If you are not reaching your goals, then ask, "What are the obstacles? What do I have to do differently? Should I do more of the same things I currently do?"

Chapter 1: You & Your Life

Pile #53
Being Selfish in Your Thoughts

When we become saddened, some of us turn our anger inward and attack ourselves, and in the process, we turn our thoughts inward, as well. We forget those around us because we are worried about healing ourselves. Thoughts become inwardly focused and do not take into account those who may need us in the external world that is outside of our heads.

Sometimes, the best way of resolving sadness is to "get outside of your head," meaning that helping people may be the best way to help yourself. Forgetting your problems that you ruminate about and instead doing something active to help others, in turn, helps you.
When you are feeling *crappy*, reach out to help others and, together, you may both reach a goal of improved happiness. To adapt an old African proverb, "it takes a village" for all of us to develop (and maintain) our happiness.

Pile #54
Saying You're Sorry to Everything

Have you ever noticed that when children get in trouble, they are quick to say sorry? Ask them what they are sorry for, and they will often say they don't know. The apologies were simply a kneejerk reaction because they have learned what they think adults want to hear.

As adults, we sometimes emulate this by apologizing for anything that we believe may remotely offend someone, or merely out of habit. Doing so undermines your assertiveness, your honesty, and even your reputation.

When you are wrong, apologize. When you are not, or if you don't need to, don't.

Chapter 2
Technology & Your World

"I fear the day that technology will surpass our human interaction. The world will have a generation of idiots."
- (Falsely attributed to Albert Einstein)

We have become like moths drawn to a flame. If you look up at the world around you, chances are you will see more people looking down than meeting your gaze. Our generation(s) have become attracted to the soft white glow of smartphones, tablets, and computer monitors over the face-to-face conversations of the world.

A few years ago, we would become angry and frustrated when we had to leave a message or speak with a machine instead of a human being. Now, it is the norm. In fact, for some there is a great deal of relief when they do not have to engage in small talk with a living, breathing person.

With the World Wide Web, our world is getting ever smaller. You can now reach far-off lands with a few simple clicks of the mouse. Yet our world seems more distant than ever, as teenagers stand shoulder-to-shoulder, texting away. Adults glare down at a screen when they are out to dinner, only to look up to see where their next bite of food is coming from or if they have a child acting up.

Social media has placed us in a world in which we try to embellish our lives more than the next person, and relationships are based on how many "friends" you have on social media versus who you could invite out for lunch or dinner. Our relationships have devolved from happy, three-dimensional communications to crappy, flat, one-dimensional interactions that take place through the tip-tapping of keyboards and a monitor screen.

So, this section talks about how to survive the world of technology, and about how it can sap your relationships from happiness and pull you into the computerized, binary world of *crappiness*.

Pile #1
Believing All the "Fake News" of Social Media

In the frenetic onslaught of information that is the internet, we hear a lot about "fake news." That is, news stories which seem to come from legitimate sources, about topics that seem reasonable enough, but have little or no foundation in reality.

People debate, of course, regarding the source of these materials. They maintain an ongoing dialogue of what is true, how true the truth is, and who quoted whom. Now, I am not talking about these "fake news" stories when I discuss this topic. Rather, I am addressing how we edit, cut, and splice our own social media pages to make our world and lives seem vastly more interesting than they really are.

Do you ever notice that some people can't just make a dinner? No, on social media it becomes a gourmet meal. They do not just go on a family vacation—they go on a family voyage that would make those on reality dating shows jealous. It makes one wonder—do they ever do anything mundane, like get takeout and watch a movie on demand?

Of course, they do. However, that drab film of their lives is left on the "cutting room floor" of their social media accounts. No-one wants to read or watch that and, let's face it—it is boring and humdrum. Only the most interesting content (or what we can make seem interesting) is destined for the ultimate film that details our lives via social media walls.

The issue is that when we enter the doors of a social media site, we are barraged with everyone who polishes their information to make their lives look as entertaining as possible. Then we gaze at our dull or lonely lives and say, "Why can't I be more like them?"

I urge you to look deeper than those carefully polished and manicured walls of others' social media accounts. Recognize that there is a lot more dropped and spliced on the cutting room floor of most social media accounts than is posted for everyone to see. It is akin to when you were a child. You didn't want to hang the red, glaring Fs up on your fridge, did you? No, that treasured real estate was generally saved for only the best work that would be proudly displayed. The Fs were made for another place... the circular filing cabinet.

Pile #2
Using Texting or Internet Communications to Convey Deep Conversations, Meaning or Feelings

Texting has become its own language. Words and feelings have now been abbreviated and symbolized. Emotions (such as *crappy* or *happy*) have now been boiled down to a picture on the tiny screen of a smartphone.

If you find that your communications are not of sufficient quality and do not provide the happiness that you desire, ask yourself—how often are my communications technological versus truly personal? The issue with technology is it takes an imperative piece out of the interactional puzzle. According to Dr. Albert Mehrabian, "7% of any message is conveyed through words, 38% through certain vocal elements, and 55% through nonverbal foundations."[10]

This means that only 7% of the substance of your conversations on the internet and over texts gets through. The remaining 93% is left up to the recipient's own subjective thoughts. That does not provide for much in the realm of clear dialogue. If you are someone who leans more toward the "*crappy*" versus the "*happy*" perspective in communications, what side do you think this virtual back-and-forth will lead to in your relationships? Naturally, a negative slant on this dialogue can be gleaned, even if that was never how you meant it.

---

[10] "Ubiquity: The 7% Rule." *Acm - an Acm Publication*, ubiquity.acm.org/article.cfm?id=2043156.

Pile #3
Relationships That Seem Too Good to Be True

One of the best ways to develop happiness, many of us believe, is through fostering an intimate relationship or friendship. We spend a great deal of our time dreaming about that "knight in shining armor" or the "princess in the castle." In doing so, we fill in the blanks of our lofty expectations for the person in front of us to meet.

The challenge with relationships over the internet is that so much of these interactions can be manufactured. You can Photoshop your profile picture or, alternatively, just use someone else's. You can lie about your job, age, criminal record— anything and everything. Some of these may be "little white lies" such as shaving a few years off your age, whereas others may be significantly more serious. I daresay most slant things to portray what they want others to believe about them.

Often the more seriously skewed profiles are known as "catfishing". The process, should you be unfamiliar with it, is one in which a person totally fabricates a profile and goes out to "fish "for a lonely, unsuspecting person. Once an unwitting victim is "hooked", the catfish sets about getting money or material goods (sometimes to the tune of thousands). You may say, "How can someone be so gullible?"

In our search for happiness, we use emotion, not logic, and develop a single focused vision for a relationship that does not exist. It becomes like a drug—in the short term, it fosters happiness, but over the longer haul it creates crappiness when we lie to ourselves in an ever deeper capacity.

Pile #4
Looking Down Can Get You Down

As I suggested earlier in this chapter, look at those around you.

It seems that the world has become hypnotized by the lure of the internet. Family dinners are monopolized by people checking their social media feeds, children are babysat at the restaurant with tablets, and teens text away at lightning speed.

In all the looking down, however, we forget to even glance up. Looking up at those relationships that can be developed in front of us is a neglected art. According to the website Changing Minds, as well as a host of researchers on friendships/relationships, the following are key to fostering and enriching interactions into potential relationships:

- *Similarity*: How much we have in common with others.
- *Proximity*: How often we see and meet others around us.
- *Reciprocity*: How much we like each other.

When these factors are met, they greatly increase the chances of a positive coupling, be it friendship or a more intimate partnership. The issue, though, is that when you are looking down at technology, you tend to neglect the potential interactions directly in front of you. Those who can perhaps bring you happiness may literally be right in front of you, but are crowded out in favor of the latest e-mail or text being pushed into your smartphone.

Pile #5
Looking Down at the Screen and Missing the Here and Now

One of the most certain ways to generate more anxiety and less happiness is to not be "present-centered" in all aspects of your life—that is, being unable to remain focused on the "here and now". If you cannot stay in the gift of the present, you will perpetually stare behind or in front of you while missing what is right next to you. You become like someone who is farsighted, and trip over the items closest to you because they are out of your field of vision.

When you type away on social media about how great a time you are having, how can you remain present, fully appreciating that moment? The short answer is that you can't—you are distracted and glaring down while you miss the world around you because the internet/smartphone/tablet places a barrier between you and experiencing things fully.

Think about it—would you rather do a web search for a trip to the Caribbean, or be there? To develop maximum happiness and experience people, places, and things, you must truly be there 110%. Pictures and videos are great mementos—just don't let technology be a barrier to fully absorbing the life that is out there for you.

Pile #6
Allowing Yourself No Escape

Not so many years ago, if you wanted to escape the long arm of your employer, you could simply leave work or home and they could not bother you in the oasis that was the outside world. Then came beepers, followed by cellular phones and, finally, smartphones.

Many of us have jobs wherein communication is critical on a regular basis. That, unfortunately, is an unavoidable job responsibility assigned under the nebulous title, "those not otherwise listed." However, how many of us have replied to an endless barrage of emails that were not of important or critical nature and hence kept us chained to our jobs 24/7? Is it important that someone knows what you want for lunch on Monday?

The vast majority of emails in most jobs are not emergencies. Yet, as is human nature, when an email comes through it is almost impossible not to read it. What does it say? Who is it from? What do they want? And so, every email becomes an emergency.

But again, if everything is an emergency, nothing becomes an emergency. If everything is a priority, nothing is a priority.

Consider finding a time to shut off your email or limit responding. By replying to petty emails, you teach others that your free time is not valuable. Moreover, you are telling them that they take priority over your family, friends and leisure time (the "*happy*, not *crappy*" times of your life). Additionally, on email programs, you can prioritize certain email accounts that should be highlighted for you to expeditiously address.

Pile #7
Believing the Grass is Greener on the Other Side of the Internet

When we are on the web, relationships are badly skewed. As we mentioned before, people edit their lives to make them seem exciting, and their reputations to be pristine and utterly utopian.

This is coupled with the temptation of not having to deal with reality, like bills or kids. It is so easy to be drawn into the falsehoods of social media and believe the grass on the vast pastures of the World Wide Web to be greener than it is in your present situation.

What this leads to, however, is a comparison against an unrealistic, fantastical standard. Chances are, in the long run, you will be far happier addressing the issues in front of you than you would be in yearning and searching to find comparable happiness in the World Wide Web.

Pile #8
Searching for Love in All the Wrong Places

Literally billions of people are on social media. Many find social media to be the best way to "cast a wide net" into the web and catch a relationship. The issue is that social media was never truly designed for that sole purpose.

Yes, social sites were initially designed to socialize. However, social media was never solely intended to be a dating platform. As a result, the fish you reel in may not be of the quality or type you want. Why? Because why would you fish in a pond where the water is not pre-cleaned or filtered?

Online dating certainly has its place, and more people than ever are finding love that way. Just keep in mind that online dating sites are the place for that activity, not a social site. These sites are the ones that actively filter, research to find the right matches, and give you a far better chance than you'd have trying to find someone in the "meat market" of most social media sites.

Pile #9
Being Too Comfortable

There is no doubt that the internet is a comfortable means of communication for most of us. We can display our points of view toward others, or even say things we would never say to someone in person (this is how cyberbullying partially got its rise) all while sitting on our couch in our pajamas.

There is a certain comfort to not having to meet up with people, to typing rather than talking. With internet communication, there is far less chance of being hurt emotionally because the bonds you form are not quite as strong as they would be in person-to-person interaction.

In short, there is a comfortable distance for most people, an ability to communicate without leaving the comfort of their homes or emotional confines. Just remember that "comfortable" doesn't always mean *happy*. Many people stay in bad or uncomfortable relationships because "they know the devil they got and are not sure of what they could get." In turn, one settles into a "good enough," even when that good enough is actually terrible. Nevertheless, the emotions are still real.

Chapter 3
You and Others...
Relationships from *Crappy to Happy*:

Without a doubt, relationships with others are an integral key to happiness. Not just any relationships, however—quality bonds are necessary for you to build and preserve your happiness. Conversely, keeping negative associations in your life knocks you down repeatedly and leaves you exhausted and emotionally barren.

Many of us tend to settle in the quality control department of the connections of our lives. When we choose this shortcut strategy, our marriages, families, and self-esteem suffer. Many an unneeded worry and issue arises from spending too much time thinking of those who think little about us. We spend too much time straddling the line of juggling relations with many of those to whom we are superficially attached, and as a result, the quality of those relationships most important to us suffer.

If most people are asked what they hope for, their answer is a happy marriage, well-balanced children (if they want children), their own health and stability, and satisfaction in all aspects of their lives. Yet, the many little dings of life occupy most of our time, and cause unnecessary distraction and consternation to those at risk of missing and failing to enrich the larger picture of their lives and goals.

In this portion, we will spare the roles of marriage and parenting. Rather, we will lay down some basic ground rules for keeping happy and avoiding piles in the way you relate to the world and those in it.

Pile #1
Spending Time Gossiping

This is much like judging, except that it is done in a public forum. In judging, you may think to yourself, "Look at how that person dresses or acts." In gossiping, you bring that to a more public forum, in that you are judging and talking about someone in the domain of a group.

Gossiping, like judging, takes the onus away from improving yourself and brings it to an unproductive conversation about someone else and their faults and flaws. Additionally, those who gossip with you likely also gossip about you the second your back is turned.

To avoid gossip, simply ask yourself the following questions about what you plan to say:

- Is it true and accurate? If it is true, do you have the whole story?
- Is it necessary? If it will not spread kindness in the world, it is simply unnecessary.
- Why are you saying it? Are you saying it to better someone and their reputation? Or is it to tear someone or something down, or simply to have something to talk about?

Pile #2
Spending Time with "Debbie Downers"

There are people who can look at the glass as half full, half empty, or shattered completely. Depending on our mood, we may all lean more toward one viewpoint or another. However, there are those who are chronically negative and see the glass as perpetually broken, unable to fixed or able to hold even a drop of liquid in their cup.

If you spend a great deal of your time with these people, you will find yourself constantly pouring your cup of happiness into their glass, only to find it seeps out of the many cracks and fractures of the weak "cups" of their own psyches. No matter what you say or how much you pour, it empties out of these persons as quickly as you replenish it, until one day you find nothing in your glass, either, and echo the same negativity that you hear from the "downers" of your life.

You will encounter these people at work, in your family, in your friendships, and in every facet of your life. Though you cannot eliminate them completely, you can limit how much time you spend with them. If you are constantly trying to get someone else to see the positive side of things, it will eventually drain your own positive reserves and motivation. Select those who empower and add to your joy in life, not those who drain you of the positivity that you seek. Look for positive people who:

- Seek to build you and others up.
- Talk about the positive and productive activities rather than complaining.
- Are problem-solvers vs. problem-makers.
- Don't talk negatively about others who are not present in the conversation.

Building your self-esteem and self-worth will also increase your ability to take responsibility for your actions. Do not fear making mistakes—rather, dread making those mistakes and not learning from them.

Pile #3
Trying to Make Everyone Happy

It is impossible to make everyone happy. Even on a bright, sunny day, I'd bet the guy selling the umbrellas down the street is not so pleased.

The fact is that everyone has different motives, desires, and agendas. Sometimes the goals of those you want to please are close enough that you can satisfy all (or most) parties.

Other times, you simply cannot make everyone 100% happy. Maybe everyone will be okay with that, or maybe a few of your family/friends will say that 75% is not good enough. Then the fact you tried to do what you believed they wanted is for naught, and no-one is fully satisfied.

It is better to make yourself or those closest to you happy, if you can. Being self-centered—versus trying to make a few acquaintances happy and starving yourself and those closest to you of the emotional affection and attention that you all need—is usually a better means of ensuring happier days ahead.

Pile #4
Believing You'll Find Happiness or Satisfaction in Your Next Promotion or Job

When I was younger, my father was a hard worker. He probably would have called himself a workaholic. Still, he found time to run 5 miles daily and ate right. He paid his own way through school, eventually earning a PhD in Electrical Engineering.

In July of 1992, he had a seizure while on one of his many global business trips as a director for the Department of Defense. As it turned out, he was diagnosed with an aggressive and quickly fatal brain tumor.

Myself being a young adult, and with precious few months for him to distill a lifetime of learning into me, he decided on just a few lessons. The primary life lesson was simple—don't sacrifice family or friends solely for a life of work. No promotion, no amount of money is worth a life that is sidetracked by a constant weight of stressors that keeps you from fully enjoying a life that is too short. As the Eagles song says, you "can spend all your time making money… you can spend all your money making time." Which is more important to you, in this short time on this earth?

A job or promotion, in and of itself, will never bring happiness. Strive instead for contentment and peace in your life, along with being able to support your family. Seek balance, rather than aiming only to climb a ladder.

Pile #5
Saying Yes When You Want to Say No!

As you establish your priorities, people will tug and pull at you to re-prioritize based on their own needs and wants. The powerful two-letter word, "No," sets the boundaries necessary to foster your own happiness.

Now, you may exclaim, "People will not be happy with me—others will be disappointed." This may be true. However, I want you to imagine you are having a great day and are at 100% (most of us are never at 100% all the time). Now, you have to spread that same 100% of you among the various responsibilities of your life (such as those below):

- Family
- Friends
- Work
- Hobbies
- Spirituality/Religion
- Volunteer Work

As you spread your "100%" thinner and thinner, you slowly lose the ability to give your all to everything (or anything). The question then becomes, do you want to give a percentage of yourself to areas that are not important to you out of some blind sense of obligation? Or, more importantly, do you want to give most of yourself to those things/persons that are of vital interest to you? To whom do you want to give your motivation and energy most fully (e.g. family, friends, work)?

The choice is yours. Again, remember that you can do—and give to—anything you want, but not everything you want.

Pile #6
Saying No When You Want to Say Yes!

Similar to the last "pile" is when you say no to an opportunity because of a host of "what if" scenarios that could potentially occur, or because of anticipatory anxiety. Often, the anticipation of doing something is much worse than the act itself. It is akin to riding a rollercoaster. What is the scariest part of that ride? It is not going down those metal rails of terror—no, it is the anticipation as you hear the slow click up the hill toward that drop of doom.

It is much like when you don't say yes to what you want to incorporate into your life. Notice, I say "want to incorporate," not "feel obligated to incorporate." We create mountains of hesitation toward some of the things we most want to do and try to talk ourselves out of them. In doing so, we build ever higher hills of anticipation that become more challenging to scale each time we try to do so.

If it is safe, will not hurt anyone else, and is positive in nature, then ask yourself—what is the harm in saying yes? If the only thing stopping you is your anxiety, then the guilt and the emotional lashing you will give yourself for saying "no" is often much worse than the attempt and any potential failure.

Pile #7
Chasing After Others

Have you ever taken part in a close couple's dance? When you dance forward, your partner takes a step back. You take another step forward, they take another stride back. Now, you shift backward, and they take a step forward. And so it goes, as it also does in the dance of life.

If you always pursue and step forward after others in life, you will always be chasing and never have the opportunity to be chased. Also, you will never truly know others' loyalty if they are never given the opportunity to present their loyal nature. Relationships exist on a seesaw. That is, there are times as a friend or partner when one may need to lift a bit more of the load and then, later down the line, the other partner may pick up more than their share. In the end, it should translate to roughly even distribution within a good friendship, partnership, or relationship.

If, however, one finds themselves carrying the bulk of the relationship most of the time, they may now have to examine the situation in a more skeptical light. Chasing after relationships says more about you than it does the other person. Imagine a garden in which all you do is water and feed the weeds that grow there. Yet, in your efforts, you neglect all the beautiful flowers and delicious vegetables because your focus is solely on the weeds. The flowers and vegetables end up withering away. Feed and water what, and whom, you want in your life—don't chase after what you think you need to validate yourself.

Pile #8
Attempting to be a Mind Reader

It is human nature to try to find a purpose, a pattern, or a reason for everything. Sometimes on the internet you will find that people attempt to sell a piece of toast or a vegetable that "looks" like a famous character or symbol for some astronomical price. They may see an image in a piece of toast or on a cracker that "looks like" it has the silhouette of someone famous. The point is, we are masters at finding or deriving meaning from things that are seemingly meaningless.

Psychology has a name for this—*apothecia*.[11] The term means finding/seeking a pattern (or patterns) when one does not actually exist. As people, we always try to fill in the blanks that exist in a vacuum of seeming meaninglessness. It is a critical aspect of human nature to need explanation—we need answers, and will pull them out of midair, if necessary.

We often fill in those same blanks regarding people's thoughts and motives. The problem is that we are

---

[11] "Apophenia." *Wikipedia*, Wikimedia Foundation, 5 Dec. 2017, en.wikipedia.org/wiki/Apophenia.

often wrong. According to psychologist Dr. William Ickes, who has studied this topic, we "read" each other with an average accuracy rate of only 20%. With those we know well, such as a partner, the number rises to a mere 35%, and it is extremely rare for anyone to score at or above 60% overall.[12] This means that when you assume someone's motivation for doing something that you perceive is against you and causes you sadness and angst, guess what? You may be at least partially wrong about their motivation (a majority of the time).

You may have heard that you need to constantly reassure children that a divorce (or other negative adult event) was not their fault. Why is that? Because children are egocentric little beings. They look at the world and say, "This place revolves around me, so everything that happens, or does not happen, somehow is a direct result of my behavior." Of course, we know that the world is far more complex than that, and everyone has different goals, beliefs, and desires. In fact, we are all just a tiny part of a system that is massive beyond our comprehension.

---

[12] "Everyday Mind Reading." *Psychology Today*, Sussex Publishers, www.psychologytoday.com/blog/everyday-mind-reading.

Or do we truly know that? For you see, many of us are upset because of something we perceive that someone has done directly to us. In reality, it is not that they did something to us—it is that they did something without *thinking* about us. Their harsh or seemingly mean-spirited actions that we believe were *against us* are due more to the fact they *simply did not think about us*, our feelings, needs, or concerns.

Now the vital question is, "What do I do about that and the hurt I feel?" The answer is, ask the person for clarification of their feelings or motives. You will feel much better if you immediately understand their thought process than if you leave your own speculations to brew and fester like weeds in your brain as to what you think the motives *may* have been. After all, how often do you surmise those motivations to be positive inside your own head? Most often, they ferment into negative and angry thoughts of how you were wronged and deeply hurt.

Pile #9
Expecting Others to Read YOUR Mind

Now that we understand we are not so great at reading the minds of others, what does that say about another person's ability to read yours? Let's say that you have a long-term partner, old friend, spouse, etc.

Too often, we think, "They should always know what I need, feel, want… if they *REALLY* know me." We play the "silent game" where we indicate nothing is wrong and leave the other person to play a game of charades to figure out what is bothering us, and then we become aggravated because they are wrong, or not totally on the mark, or ignore our tacit desires.

If you need something, ***say it***. If you want something, ***ask for it***. If you feel something, ***express it***. The formula is simple, but often we forego this template, making it infinitely more complex in the dialogue of relationships with others. It leads us to not being happier because we feel misunderstood. If you want to be recognized, communicate what you want.

Pile #10
Expecting to Get Back What You Give

If you are a giver—that is, someone who always does everything for everybody and then is frustrated and saddened because it is not reciprocated in equal measure—here is a question… Why are you *truly* giving?

You may say, "Because I am a good person," or "Because I like to help others." There are many possible reasons why you may be a giver. Please know, being a giver is a great thing. It is your kindness that makes the world a wonderful place and makes us human.

Ask yourself, however, *truly* why do you give? Is it to get something in return? If you give to get something in return, you are not giving—you are engaging in a transaction. Think about it—you are giving them your kindness, your time, your money in hopes of getting them to return something to you. Ever wonder why people give away millions anonymously? They want to be certain that they are giving and not expecting anything in return.

Don't get me wrong—it is hurtful to get nothing back when you give and give. However, it is exhausting to keep a mental ledger of your deposits and withdrawals, isn't it? Furthermore, relationships are not merely linear—that is, they are not built upon an equal measure of give and take. Ever notice how sometimes the people from whom you expect the least do the most for you in certain situations?

Relationships are an intricate web—sometimes you get more from one person than another. Other times, you give more to one person than another. Trying to keep track of every one at once will leave you bitter, resentful, and quite a bit *crappier* than *happier*.

Pile #11
Expecting Others to Make You Totally Happy or Whole

Most of us have heard the time-tested adage, "You must love yourself before you can love anyone else." Now, I am not certain if you have to fully love everything about yourself to enter into a satisfying relationship—however, you do have to like and care for yourself.

If you do not, you simply hook yourself to someone else's star. This is even a harder road to tow than not liking yourself. Why? Because now you are attaching your emotional well-being to someone else's less predictable, or more volatile, star. If they are sad, you are sad. If you have disappointed them, you have disappointed yourself. In short, you look for them to make you whole. This means you cannot regulate yourself emotionally because you have given them your emotional thermostat.

Happiness comes from believing in yourself and your accomplishments jointly, as well as your achievements independently. It cannot come solely from constantly supporting someone else's accomplishments on top of your own.

Pile #12
Not Saying What You Wish You Had Said When You Could Have Said It

Often life gets extremely complicated—we become bogged down in the muddy muck of life and forget what we are going to do the next moment, let alone the next day. We forget to thank those who have been kind to us, who have mentored us, and to make amends with those close to us whom we have wronged or who have wronged us.

Take time once a month (or more) to write a note or a text, make a phone call, or "do lunch" to thank those who have helped you or resolve issues that are pressing on your mind. Doing so will help take the *crappier* days and make them happier, as well as clean up some of the *crappier* issues of negative relationships.

Pile #13
Holding a Grudge

Have you ever had a person that you really can't stand? I mean a person that really brings out the very worst in you. This is the person you have nightmares about at night, you rant about in the day, and the slightest thought of them makes your blood boil.

Think about the power you have given to that person. Imagine they are somewhere by a pool, relaxing, sipping a cool drink, and meanwhile they have a vice grip on you wherever they go. They are not thinking about you, but thinking about them is all that you *can* do. It is as though you have given them the remote control for your mind and freely allowed them to channel surf.

Sure, you may try to cut them out of your life by not talking with them, or limit your contact. The question is, have you truly cut them off if you still have such strong emotions bubbling like lava in the pit of your stomach? You have cut communicational but not emotional ties with them. Often those emotional ties are much stronger and connective than mere proximity.

You must wrestle with the fact that you need to let the situation go. You may call it forgiveness or simply "letting it go." A lot of people equate forgiving with forgetting, but in reality, to forgive and merely forget is quite naïve. If I forget that you tried to beat me over the head with a bat, not only am I naïve, but it is generally not the best strategy for my long-term survival.

But grappling and some form of forgiveness or moving on is, in fact, necessary. First, acknowledge your feelings. You may say, "My feelings are of anger, hatred, or bitterness." Look deeper than that, because the emotion of anger is an "iceberg emotion"—meaning that, if you look at the surface, you merely see the tip, which is anger. If you look below the surface, you will see a much broader root of fear, sadness, disappointment, shame, etc. Focus on those deeper feelings instead.

Sure, you may want to use profanity to describe that sh**head or a**hole who wronged you. Avoid that, not because you don't feel that way, but because profane language simply does not help clarify or explain a situation. After all, is your sh**head the same sh**head as the one I deal with? Or, here's a better question—are all sh**heads equal? No—be specific in describing what bothers you about what they did, and what is wanted to remedy the issue.

Try to see, really *see*, why they did it. Once we feel someone has greatly wronged us, they cease to be a person in our minds. They become a profanity, and anything they may have done or will do is always viewed in that most negative light. Is it possible that the way you saw the situation/issue is even slightly askew?

Write to them about how you feel. Don't worry if it seems strange or doesn't make as much sense as you would like. The important thing is to write a letter of what has angered you. Be specific, and be just as detailed regarding what you would like them to do about it. Make certain if you have some part in the issue (in relationships, there are always at least two sides) that you address that, too. Now, read it. Putting it on paper sometimes helps to make sense of the jumble of emotions and anger that have resulted from all the pent-up resentment.

Pile #14
Fear of Disappointing Others

As previously stated in Chapter 3, is impossible to make everyone happy, and trying to do so will often result in hurt and frustration. Thus, it is not worthwhile for you to base all your decisions on the fear of failing to meet others' unmanageable list of expectations.

Do what you feel is right or best for you and the priorities and values that matter to you. People may not always like them—however, you can sleep at night and know you have been true to yourself and your beliefs.

Pile #15
Judging Others

We all have a natural inclination to judge others. We watch, compare, and decide others' lifestyles, cultures, and thoughts are counter to ours. This allows us to judge them and spend emotional energy criticizing, belittling, or gossiping about how those persons don't compare based upon some standard that we have established within our own flawed lifestyle.

More importantly, judging leads down a path of anger and negative emotion that is directed toward others. In short, it places our emotional well-being in a place that is not helpful for us. Also, it creates an atmosphere in which we do not focus on improving ourselves and our own well-being because we are too busy pointing out the flaws in others. Either way, we are the *crappiest* version of ourselves when we focus on tearing others down versus finding an opportunity to build up our own lives.

Additionally, judging often leads to looking toward others in a negative fashion. "Those people are that way." "He/she always is like that—they always get what they want." "They are jerks, a**holes, bastards, b**ches." Your current tone or mood may change what you say or think about that person and the world around you.

Pile #16
Not Recognizing Adult Bullies

In the playground of life, there will always be bullies. Little bullies can grow up to be big bullies, and they can knock those in their adult playground for a loop. Be aware of those who push their agenda at the expense of your own or those of others close to you. If you do not set boundaries for your own happiness, they will quickly take over and invade those limits. If you give these bullies an inch, they will take a mile, as well as your dinner, your job, and whatever else is there for the grabbing in the basket of life. Asserting what is yours strongly, often, and early without stepping down to their level of aggression will save headaches and *crappiness* later down the line.

Pile #17
Trusting But Verifying

In life, Benjamin Franklin said, "A fool and his money are soon parted." We all know things that are "too good to be true." Whether they be on social media, job openings, or financial investments, false opportunities abound in every angle of the world.

Yet, we try to talk ourselves into them by minimizing certain aspects, not following our gut instinct, or just not listening to naysayers.

Before you trust and engage in something that is too good to be true, wait. Dip your toe in—doing so allows you to look and research whether what you are being told is relatively accurate. Listen to others and your instincts, as well. Remember that a salesman (of any profession or in the game of life) has a job, and that is to sell. If one embellishes the truth (or even tells a small lie), what is the harm in his philosophy on engagement? The harm to you is that it can lead you down a road that leaves you crawling out for months, or years, and leave you kicking yourself because you did not validate what you were told.

Pile #18
Using Middle School Strategies as Adults and in the World

Think back to middle school—everything was a popularity contest. It is a world of constant comparisons of who is more popular, who has more friends, better sneakers, and more fashionable clothes. It is also (as previously mentioned) a world in which drama energizes the atmosphere, and preteens are rewarded by peers for finding new, creative ways to channel that drama for attention-seeking.

Flash forward a decade or two, and you should (ideally) recognize that this world of popularity is a mere façade. Friendships are not judged by number, but quality. We are not awarded for more drama (unless you are a professional actor). Plus, using these immature habits will make you feel far *crappier* in a world that has matured around you. Some "adults" never evolve past this stage.

When you make choices throughout the day, ask yourself, "Can I put my head on the pillow at night over this decision?" In other words, do the choices I make (or feel forced to make) align with my personal values and ethics, or am I doing things because I am told to do them, or out of blind allegiance to someone else? Remember, it is likely better to say no than to go against your own principles, beliefs, and character. Those who "just follow orders" are often the ones who are swept into crises and lumped together with those whose course of action may not be consistent with their ethical beliefs.

Pile #19
Watering the Weeds and Not the Flowers

In 1960, a journalist name Gordon Young asked historical psychologist Carl Jung about what factors are necessary for human happiness. Among the ones Dr. Jung emphasized were, "Good personal and intimate relationships, such as those of marriage, the family, and friendships." Research efforts over the last fifty years in all branches of mental health and medicine have reached similar conclusions—relationships are the key factor to happiness throughout an individual's lifetime.

Yet, we tend to neglect these relationships and friendships due to being stretched in every direction by a bevy of other obligations. In turn, we water and feed all the other elements of our lives and leave our precious relationships to wither on the vine of good intentions.

So, with life becoming ever busier, and knowing that relationships lead to a *happier* condition, how do you maintain them?

- Text, call, or email close friends at least once or twice a week: This may seem overwhelming, but a quick call, email, or text lets them know that you're thinking of them.

Simply scheduling interactions with one or two people per week with your smartphone calendar and then setting that event for "recurring" will allow you to do this with little time or effort.

- Remember the little and big things: If your friend or family member is having a big medical test, a promotion, having a baby, etc. make sure you document those items and check in just to let them know that you care.

- Birthdays are vital: Send a card—not an email, text, or social media message. Sending a card shows you took the time to write something, and is different from the barrage of emails and texts that one gets on a regular basis.

- Pruning friendships: All of us change and evolve in our lives. Some of those who grow into our lives also grow out. They may not be in the same stage of life (with spouses, children, etc.) or may have different interests. If this is the case, you simply and gradually grow apart. You cannot equally feed all friendships, so consider pruning the ones you can't in favor of growing the ones you can and want to maintain.

- You are an adult friend and a parent: If you are a parent, remember that you also must be an adult. That means you must also have adult friendships and relationships. Do not always sacrifice these in favor of the sole role of mother/father, husband/wife, if possible.

Chapter 4
You and Long-Term Partnerships

"Trust is the glue of life. It's the most essential ingredient in effective communication. It's the foundational principle that holds all relationships."
--Stephen Covey

As you begin this chapter, you may be a person who is single. You may say, "I don't need a spouse to be happy." That could be entirely true—you can lead a happy life independent of a significant other or kids, provided that is truly what you want. So, if that is the case, you may consider ignoring parts of this section.

However, many people find intimate, committed long-term relationships (such as marriage) and children are key factors in enriching their happiness and lives. Consequently, they can find these same relationships to be some of the most challenging of their lives. These same love-filled relationships with those moments of elation will invariably dip into segments of *crappiness*, as well.

So, we are going to look at some of the piles to avoid as you step into a committed relationship, jump into that minivan to soccer practice with your kids, and look down the road of going from a "you" to a "we," and from a self-centered identity to that of a husband, wife, and/or parent.

Pile #1
Believing Not Arguing is Better Than Not Talking to Each Other

Many of us believe that arguing is the worst element of relationships. Conflict over finances, children, and budgeting of time can be challenging and, at times, uncomfortable. We equate conflict with arguing, yelling, and screaming.

Yet, there is something much more insidious and tacitly dangerous—no energy being fed into a partnership. When a couple ignores each other, it is indicative of a lack of energy to push for conflict resolution to develop prospective solutions. Therefore, it is apathy, giving up, and a lack of energy invested in relationships that is most costly and dangerous to their long-term health.

Pile #2
Ending Relationships Too Early

When a relationship dissolves and someone quickly moves on, it is often said that they are on "the rebound." This, of course, implies that they are prematurely moving to a new potential partnership before they are fully ready.

Indeed, a "rebound" relationship can be doomed to fail if either party is not ready or healed enough to establish a new bond. To avoid a *crappy* rebound, one must do everything they can to preserve former marital relationships before concluding that they should end in divorce. Of course, cases of abuse or affairs leave a wide berth as an exception.

Doing so ensures that the guilt and regret will be dramatically reduced because one can leave the relationship with a relatively clear conscience.

Pile #3
Looking for Everything in Your Spouse

No-one can be everything for you. If that were the case, why would you need more than one friend? After all, if that single person could fulfill all those needs, the purpose of finding someone else to fill any void would be nonexistent, right?

Therefore, do not expect your significant other to fulfill every wish and need you desire. A more realistic goal is to expect them to enrich your life. It is simply too much pressure to put on a relationship to believe that the other person could do, and be, everything to you. It takes away from you as an individual, and leads to cracks in the foundation of unrealistic expectations for the long haul.

Pile #4
Being "In Love" With "Being in Love"

Brides love to plan for their weddings. Many have been dreaming of every aspect of that day since they were young girls—the flowers, the dress, and the knight in shining armor who will sweep them off their feet into a beautiful sunset overlooking some turquoise, crystal blue ocean.

Of course, the danger can often be the "devil in the details" in which all the planning goes into the wedding and the romance of the day. Subsequently, little is invested in thinking about the much more important, infinite days and years that hopefully follow.

If you know more about the groom/bride cake topper than the groom himself, or if you can interchange any guy/gal for the groom/bride because you are obsessed with the notion of marriage and love, you are more likely to fall into the category of *crappy* versus *happy*.

Pile #5
Not Having Matching Values

As the old saying goes, "Opposites attract." Or do they? In my years working with couples, I have seen many pairs who appear to be polar opposites, couples who seem to have a great deal in common, and everything between, all with varying degrees of relational satisfaction.

So, the question is, how do you have a relationship that is established more on the side of *happier* than that of *crappier*? Ah, there is the crucial, age-old question. That answer mostly seems to depend upon the following factor—despite personality traits and characteristics, are you both of the same mind when it comes to your global values?

Here are some global values to consider when seeking to take the next step into a more serious intimate relationship:

Do you agree on:

- Finances: Who handles the finances of the relationship? How do you manage credit and credit cards? Do you adhere to so-called "traditional" means of gender finances? What are your individual and partnered money goals?

- Family: How important is your extended family in your daily choices? Do you both want children? How many? What are your thoughts on how to parent, and on disciplining your children?

- Work: How important is work? What is an acceptable time ratio for your job/life balance? Is it okay if one or both of you travel for your vocation(s)? How willing are each of you to support your partner's continuing education/schooling? How stable are your respective work situations?

- Friends: Do you like each other's friends? Do you have mutual friendships or only friendships that are exclusive of each other? How do each of you feel about the other having friendships with the opposite sex? How much time should be distributed between the friend/family balance?

- Culture: If you are from differing cultures, are you respectful of your partner's culture? Do you recognize that there may be profound differences in the way you think and were brought up? Do you realize that some ways of thinking are not "right or wrong," just different from your own?

Pile #6
Getting Blamed for Being the Blamer in a Relationship

Relationships mean taking responsibility for one's own actions. Do you tend to get "blamed" completely for what goes wrong in a relationship? Or, conversely, do you solely blame the other person for what is going awry in the partnership between you?

If you are to be successful, it will require both mature individuals to recognize that they each have a balance in what ultimately happens to both members of the couple. If you cannot recognize the part you play in the relationship, it becomes hard not to resent the other person's flaws and faults. "It takes two to tango," so to speak, and it also takes two to engage fully in a relationship.

Pile #7
Starting a Relationship Off "Behind the Eight Ball"

Marriage is not always easy. Over a lifetime, you face many ups and downs on the road of life, and it can be difficult enough just to keep the car from veering off the asphalt into the trees and ditches. Therefore, if you start off a relationship with issues of affairs, addiction, or abuse, you are trying to start a partnership on the foundation of a relational mudslide.

We frequently try to convince ourselves (and others) that we could "work through" these difficult challenges. Maybe it is because of a child out of wedlock, or the driving passion of love. Sometimes the reality is that love may be enough to carry you over the threshold of being a bride and groom, but not the threshold of life.

Abuse, alcohol, and addiction issues are not generally spousal issues (though they can be present in both partners). Usually, they are issues that the individual must remedy before they are ready to enter marriage in a mature and open manner, not after they have committed. These often become "relational deal-breakers" because one has not developed enough of themselves personally to succeed relationally.

138

Pile #8
Different Names, Same Person

If you find that you have continual relational issues with those you pursue for intimate relationships, then it is time to reevaluate you, not them. What is it that you are looking for (or not looking for) in these relationships that are not bringing the partnership to the next level? Are you looking for those who don't want to commit due to fear of rejection for yourself? Are you secretly not ready for/not interested in a long-term relationship or afraid you will fail? Do you seek to overthink and look for minor flaws versus major strengths in others so that you can immediately dismiss them? Are you recreating your own parents' dysfunctional relationship in hopes of repairing the past?

Regardless of these questions, if your relationships consistently fall apart and you keep hearing the same reasons cited, it is time to stop looking at others and honestly reevaluate yourself and your strategies (more can be found on this in my other book, _Don't Marry a Lemon_, published by Train of Thought Press).

Pile #9
Trying Not to Hurt Anyone's Feelings

Now, I am not saying to intentionally go out and hurt others' feelings. That is reckless and mean-spirited, and I suspect that you would not be reading this book if you thought otherwise.

Rather, I am talking about the many potential obligations and commitments that come down the pike for you to negotiate. Oftentimes, we try to tell "little white lies" so as to not offend or hurt another person's feelings when we simply cannot, or don't want to, commit to an activity or request. Making empty promises or excuses only serves to create more anxiety, as you have to remember how/why you said what you said and to whom. Furthermore, doing so erodes the level of trust that you have with others (especially if they find what you said to be blatantly untrue) and increases anxiety as you try to remember who you told what.

It is far easier to simply state—in a tactful fashion—that you cannot commit. You are not obligated to go into any more detail to explain why you cannot be at a party or event. It is polite to respond, but unnecessary to elaborate beyond providing a short, honest response. Doing so allows you to keep your dignity, honesty, and respect intact in the situation.

Pile #10
Expecting Your Relationships to Always Be 50/50

When we enter a relationship, we anticipate that both parties will take an equal share of the relational load. However, that is nearly impossible. First off, how do you measure 50/50?

Secondly, relationships evolve and change, and so rather than think "50/50" (which will just lead you to be disenchanted and feel *crappy*), think of effective relationships as a relational seesaw. When one person is in need or has a lot on their plate, the other may take up more than 50% of the load (and vice versa). That is the meaning of a truly effective and evolving partnership—it is dynamic and constantly changing and moving. It is generally not 50/50, and if it is, it doesn't stay that way for long. It shifts back and forth, and in the end, makes both partners happier in the balance that one calls life.

Pile #11
Allowing Triangles to Form in Your Relationships

Often when we have difficulties in our relationships, we reach out to a "third party" to address or discuss the relationship with us. This leads to the communication between both partners in the relationship itself becoming murky and unclear.

If you have an issue with someone, it is better to "hear it from the horse's mouth" rather than recruit someone as a mediator and muddy the message. If you cannot, that is when a therapist (especially a family therapist) may be more effective than an invested third party.

The difficulty arises when someone who is wrapped up in the relationship between you and the other person becomes the messenger. Generally, no one can tell your message more clearly than you.

Pile #12
Dancing with the Partner Who Does Not Want to Dance

When you dance with someone, it is a choreography of you and the other person both taking careful steps. When you step forward, they step back. Conversely, when you step back, they step forward. Likewise, if you rest your hands against another person and push, you will likely be met with another push equal to the force you apply.

So it is with relationships. If you are constantly pursuing another person, that puts them in position to take steps backward and not contribute in moving the relationship forward. If you take a step back by not constantly pursuing them, you see whether they are willing and able to take a step forward and contribute in the mutual relationship.

What if they don't take that step forward? Well, then they may not be ready (or willing) to perform the dance with you. It may be time to reflect and see if they want you as a dancing partner in either the world of friendship or a romantic partnership.

Pile #13
Believing a Relationship Without Constant Passion is a Poor Relationship

With the advent of reality television and social media comparisons, romance novels, and movies, there is a belief that constant white-hot passion and romance are a necessary and vital component of any healthy, complete relationship.

Let's examine this thought via an analogy. If we set a campfire, the belief is that the bigger and more dramatic the fire, the better. Unfortunately, the grander the fire, the quicker it will consume the wood and, ultimately, burn itself out. Comparatively, if you look at the white-hot, glowing core, you will notice that it lasts until the very end. In addition to being the longest-lasting flame, it is also the hottest.

It is much the same way in relationships. If you seek continuous passion, your relationship may well burn itself out quickly. How can you maintain constant passion when you are working, have the flu, or have tried repeatedly and done everything from a sexual vantage point? No, it takes a partnership—liking who the person is, as well as what they look like and the romance they bring with them.

Conclusion:

"Life isn't about finding yourself.
Life is about creating yourself."
--George Bernard Shaw

If you spend your life looking down for the potential "piles" you may step in, you will miss the opportunity to look up, feel the sun, and see the view. In contrast, if you find yourself stepping in every "pile" of life that there is, you will find yourself dragging the *crap* of life into every single situation of your life. As a result, your relationships, your job, and your own well-being will be plagued with the lingering aroma of *crappiness* wherever you go.

Ideally, this is a balance. If you hope to succeed in this life and achieve ultimate happiness, you cannot walk around with the fear, anticipation, or worry of the "piles" of life. Rather, remember your inherent instincts must be trusted (or at least listened to) more often. We often don't listen to our honest selves. Rather, we try to manipulate, minimize, or rationalize our ways to step around the hardships of our lives, or those things we don't want to hear or face.

When you manipulate yourself, you fall headlong into the "piles" of life. For you see, if you are not honest with yourself, most others won't be frank with you, either. Many people go through life just trying not to create any ripples or waves in relationships. In turn, they will tell you what you want to hear simply to preserve a relationship or to avoid an argument.

The problem with this is that you never grow, and the conflict still exists. If you want to learn how to get better—or, put another way, to avoid the "piles" of life—then you must, in fact, receive honest and open criticism. If the world tells you, "Hey, you are doing perfect—no worries! Keep on doing what you're doing!" then you will follow that advice, never grow, and never learn how to get better and avoid those "piles" that you continuously tread underfoot.

If there is one way this book may help you, it is in your own honesty with yourself. If you have an issue from which you want to grow and learn, be honest. Don't be harsh—that does nothing but flush your self-esteem down the proverbial toilet. Be constructive and honest concerning what you need to learn, how you can learn it, and who might mentor you along the way.

Conclusion

As we leave our time together here, please know I wish you the best in getting the sunshine of happiness upon your face, the calm breeze through your hair, and the heels of your shoes free from the "piles of *crap*" that are scattered like mines across this pasture we call life as you pursue the joy you deserve.

Thank you for spending this time with me.

About the Author:

Brett Novick lives in Ocean County, New Jersey with his wife of twenty-one years, Darla, and his two children, Billy (19) and Samantha (14).

Mr. Novick holds a Bachelor's degree in Psychology from LaSalle University in Philadelphia, PA and a Master's Degree in Family Therapy from Friends University in Wichita, KS as well as post-degree work and certification in School Social Work from Monmouth University in West Long Branch, NJ, and in Educational Leadership. Mr. Novick is licensed as a Marriage and Family Therapist, and State-Certified as a School Social Worker.

Mr. Novick has worked as a School Social Worker/Counselor for the last sixteen years and is an adjunct instructor at Rutgers University in New Brunswick, New Jersey. Additionally, he has been a licensed and Marriage and Family Therapist in private practice, community mental health, and substance abuse settings over the last twenty years. Novick has supervised in family counseling, school counseling, and centers for abused and neglected children as well as adults with developmental disabilities.

He has also authored articles in several national and international publications ranging from family therapy, to parenting a child with autism, to educational leadership.

Mr. Novick has authored three books—*Parents and Teachers Working Together* and *The Likeable, Effective, and Productive Educator*, *The Balanced Child: Teaching Children Social Skills & Character Building* all published by Rowman and Littlefield. He also authored the children's book *Brain Bully: "Standing Up to Anxiety & Worry"* published by Childswork/Childsplay and its companion game by the same title.

He has been humbled with numerous awards for his work in education, inclusive education, counseling, character education, and human rights. Those rewards include the NJEA Martin Luther King Jr. Human and Civil Rights Award, the NJSCA Ocean County School Counselor of the Year Award, the Ocean County Mental Health Advocate Award, the NJ Council on Developmental Disabilities Community Award, the NJ DOE Holocaust Memorial Hela Young Award, the NJ DOE Inclusive Educator of the Year & Exemplary Educator Awards, the NJSCA Human Rights Advocate Award, the ETS/Kids Bridge Character Educator of the Year

Award, and the U.S. Congressional Recognition for Community Service.